Judges, Decision Making and Empathy

Insights from the Bench

Mateusz Stępień and
Ewa Wilczek-Rużyczka

Routledge
Taylor & Francis Group
LONDON AND NEW YORK

First published 2025
by Routledge
4 Park Square, Milton Park, Abingdon, Oxon OX14 4RN

and by Routledge
605 Third Avenue, New York, NY 10158

Routledge is an imprint of the Taylor & Francis Group, an informa business

This book was developed as part of the research project "Empathy as a Challenge: The Example of Polish Judges," funded by the National Science Centre, Poland (project no. 2019/33/B/ HS5/01664).

British Library Cataloguing-in-Publication Data
A catalogue record for this book is available from the British Library

ISBN: 978-1-032-90213-5 (hbk)
ISBN: 978-1-032-90214-2 (pbk)
ISBN: 978-1-003-54658-0 (ebk)

DOI: 10.4324/9781003546580

Typeset in Galliard
by Apex CoVantage, LLC

Judges, Decision Making and Empathy

This book presents empirical research uncovering the views and experiences of Polish judges regarding the utilization of empathy in their work. Although there is growing interest in the role of empathy in judicial decision-making, there is little research on how judges themselves approach this issue. This volume offers an alternative to the usual focus on common law jurisdictions. It adopts a perspective that underscores the impact of professional pressures on judges' empathic abilities, leading to a form of "empathy labor" influenced by the unique characteristics of the judicial profession. It offers an in-depth examination of judges' opinions, collected through an empirical study involving in-depth interviews. The narrative delves into real cases and judicial behaviors discussed by judges, providing reference to relevant literature from other jurisdictions. The core finding of the study reveals that while judges may differ in their approaches to empathy in a judicial context, many of their practices and strategies can be linked to empathy-like phenomena. The findings also substantiate the claim that empathy used by judges is not the same as judicial empathy, which covers empathic abilities integrated into performing the judicial role. This applied theoretical perspective of "empathy labor" offers an intriguing view of how the occupational context influences judges' empathic inclinations throughout their careers. In addition to demonstrating how judges understand the role of empathy in their work, the book outlines a scenario for empathy training based on their experiences and expectations. Presenting an original approach to studying the role of empathy in judicial decision making, the book will be of interest to academics and researchers working in the areas of philosophy of law, legal theory, sociology of law, psychology of law, and emotions studies.

Mateusz Stępień is Professor at the Jagiellonian University, Krakow, and Head of the Department of Sociology of Law.

Ewa Wilczek-Rużyczka is Professor at the Andrzej Frycz Modrzewski Krakow University, and Dean of the Faculty of Psychology, Pedagogy, and Humanities.

Routledge Research in Legal Philosophy

Moral Pluralism and the Complexity of Punishment
The Penal Philosophy of H.L.A. Hart
Nicolas Nayfeld

Sport, Law and Philosophy
The Jurisprudence of Sport
Miroslav Imbrisevic

Cosmopolitanism, State Sovereignty and International Law and Politics
A Theory
Jorge E. Núñez

Human Dignity, Judicial Reasoning, and the Law
Comparative Perspectives on a Key Constitutional Concept
Edited by Brett G. Scharffs, Andrea Pin, and Dmytro Vovk

Act and Omission in Criminal Law
Autonomy, Morality and Applications to Euthanasia
Roni Rosenberg

Metaethical Issues in Contemporary Legal Philosophy
A Constitutivist Approach
Edited by Stefano Bertea and Jorge Silva Sampaio

Purely Formal Legal Theory
Deontic Networks
Ottavio Quirico

Judges, Decision Making and Empathy
Insights from the Bench
Mateusz Stępień and Ewa Wilczek-Rużyczka

For more information about this series, please visit: https://www.routledge.com/Routledge-Research-in-Legal-Philosophy/book-series/RRLP

To all the judges who participated in the research that forms the foundation of this book . . .

Contents

Introduction[1]

Filling in a partial image of empathy in judging

Mateusz Stępień

The road to exploring the role of empathy in judicial decision-making

As a consequence of ongoing challenges related to (among others) legitimacy deficits, increasing societal demands, and economic constraints, democratic systems are evidencing a need for reforms of the judiciary. Importantly, the endeavor to thoroughly reconsider feasible innovations in the judicial system does not imply a departure from the fundamental values and principles associated with an independent judiciary, impartiality, or the division of powers. Instead, it involves exploring new approaches that uphold these principles while responding to the complexities of the current environment.

In recent decades, four main approaches to the reshaping of the judicial system have emerged. Importantly, they are not driven by a political agenda aimed at altering the role of judges within a liberal constitutional framework. Not part of some populist agenda, these approaches represent possible changes in organizational matters and the interactional realm, conceivably strengthening the core structure.

The first approach is the managerial, which suggests that successful measures already utilized in the business sphere can and should be applied to reorganize the court system. This involves a) introducing quantitative tools for assessing the performance of justices, b) implementing methods to measure "court client" satisfaction, c) distinguishing between judging and administrative functions, and assigning administrative tasks to managers rather than the justices themselves. Overall, the managerial approach emphasizes trial efficiency, favoring speed, quantitative analysis, and clear accountability.

Second is the technology-focused approach that highlights the transformative potential of introducing technological innovations into the judicial system. Examples of this include electronic case management systems, online court proceedings, virtual hearings, trial recordings, and even artificial intelligence

1 This book was developed as part of the research project "Empathy as a Challenge: The Example of Polish Judges," funded by the National Science Centre, Poland (project no. 2019/33/B/HS5/01664).

DOI: 10.4324/9781003546580-1

(AI)–based supportive systems for judges. Indeed, the COVID-19 pandemic significantly accelerated adoption of many such technological changes. Here, the assumption is that technology can substantially transform the judiciary.

The third approach, which is democratic, seeks to remedy the judiciary by expanding the incorporation of democratic elements into the functioning of the courts. This strategy aims to counterbalance the potential downsides of a strict professionalization of the courts, particularly in jurisdictions where judges are not elected through democratic processes. Reforms such as expanding layperson participation in judicial decision-making, rendering hearings truly public, and making courthouses more accessible to a broader public are typical democracy-enhancing solutions. However, there are more avenues to explore in this respect.

Fourth and finally, there is the skill-based approach, which is rooted in Aristotelian and other virtue-based traditions and has recently reemerged. With the aim of incrementally transforming court proceedings, it emphasizes the cultivation of skills—such as communication, interpersonal, and emotional competencies—among judges (as well as among other court personnel). The underlying idea is that equipping future judges with the necessary tools and conditions to develop these particular skills will, over time, lead to constructive changes in their behavior, demeanor, and decision-making processes. This approach underscores the importance of organizing the work of judges in a manner that fosters the development of stable, desirable qualities. It posits that the delivery of justice ultimately depends on judges possessing these relevant skills.

Considering the many intersecting aspects within these four approaches, the skill-based one holds particular appeal and is worth deeper discussion. This is especially so due to the weakening of institutional factors that traditionally safeguard the judiciary's reasonable autonomy in liberal democracies—a process associated with authoritarian or populist drifts. The rise in attacks on judges and courts as a consequence of populist claims highlights the importance of a judge's personal characteristics and qualities. Echoing Jerome Frank's suggestions (1930), understanding the role of judges' biases, prejudices, and other negative personal influences on their decision-making should not merely lead to stronger adherence to the stone-faced ideal and an emphasis on objectivity. Instead, it should translate into the systematic shaping and strengthening of desirable qualities in a judge's character. Frank reminds us that we cannot eliminate the personal element, and there is, therefore, a need to polish it. Regrettably, this lesson has not been fully embraced, and the skill-based approach has been marginalized in the West for many years.

One challenge with the skill-based approach is that the qualities, abilities, and competencies of judges are not easily reducible to tangible, measurable metrics. Moreover, there are numerous desirable judicial skills that also interact in complex ways. The skill-based approach is not self-sufficient, as the question of what counts as desirable inevitably prompts further questions about a preferred model of the adjudication process, the role of courts in the political authority structure, and more. Therefore, instead of presenting a grand theory of judicial skills (see the virtue-centered approach, e.g., Solum 2003), it is more feasible and practical to focus on individual skills, describing their roles and places within the broader context.

Certain judicial skills are less controversial and readily listed as desirable, such as patience and impartiality. However, skills related to empathy—whether seen as a distinct competency or as an umbrella term covering a set of processes—are particularly intriguing. While this is not the place to delve into the possible meanings of empathy and various pertinent issues (to be explored further in Chapter 3), it is important to note that, for readers unfamiliar with this concept, its relative newness might be perplexing. The word itself entered the English lexicon in the early 20th century, primarily as a translation of the German *Einfühlung* (Lanzoni 2018). What might not be immediately intuitive is that the original context for *Einfühlung* was the realm of art and aesthetic experiences. It was not until later that the word found its way into the vocabularies of a plethora of fields. However, if we associate the meaning of empathy with "putting oneself in another's shoes"—that is, a process through which one person comprehends another's situation or perspective or, alternatively, "emotional attuning with others"—it becomes evident that these have been part of human experience long before the coining of the term. When we examine the history of philosophical thought—for instance, David Hume's or Adam Smith's notion of sympathy, the Confucian concept of *shu* (Ames 2022), or even the Golden Rule—they all cover processes similar to what we now associate with empathy.

On the one hand, considering approximations of what empathy might be, it does nevertheless look to be useful for judges. To put it briefly, looking through someone else's eyes can, in certain circumstances, lead to a better understanding of a legal case. Moreover, acknowledging the viewpoints of others could be seen as critical for impartiality, as it can aid in reducing prejudices. Additionally, sensitive and responsive management of legal proceedings does call for acknowledgement of the emotions experienced by all parties. All these outcomes can be achieved through empathy.

However, on the other hand, empathy can be viewed as an undesirable quality for judges, with its role in the decision-making process painted in dark colors. Generally, perhaps the initial reaction of many lawyers is that "empathy" is a concept that initially seems counterintuitive in the legal world (Henderson 1987: 1576) and that "has no place in judicial decision making" (Mathis, Diriwächter 2012: 66). As Toni M. Massaro mentioned, the "popular image of lawyers is that we are committed to formal rationality. We are trained to cabin 'empathic' responses and remain steadfast in our commitment to legal principles despite emotional dissonance" (1989: 2103). Using empathy can be seen as introducing distortions into the legal process when employed by legal decision-makers. From this perspective, its influences should be tamed rather than elaborated upon, as it brings unbridled subjectivism into judging and opens decision-making processes to well-known empathy biases (such as the similarity bias, where one tends to empathize more with a person who shares similar characteristics, and the here-and-now bias, where one empathizes more with people who are present and less with those who are absent; see, e.g., Hoffman 2000: 206–213) or the reign of emotionality. From this viewpoint, the influence of empathy on legal decision-making threatens judicial impartiality, objectivity, and neutrality. In this reading, empathy in the judicial context is considered "a wild, untamed, destabilizing force that cannot coexist with the rule of law" (Bandes 2011: 105). Indeed, these claims made within the judicial context reflect broader discussions and critical voices (see Paul Bloom and Jesse Prinz) regarding the role of empathy and its centrality for morality and human cooperation.

Thus, some would include empathy in the list of desirable judicial skills, while others would view it as a vice. This book delves into the realm of empathy in judging, exploring this contested aspect of judges' skillset.

Importantly, the interest in empathy within the context of judging, which underlies this book, did not initially arise from recognizing that this is an under-researched topic with significant potential as an element of developing the skill-based approach to improve judicial systems. The primary motivation for delving into this subject was derived from previous empirical research conducted by the author of this Introduction in Cracow's (Poland) trial courts (Dudek, Stępień 2021: 105, 110, 160). During observational research initially dedicated to investigating power distance dynamics in courtrooms, certain judicial behaviors captured the researchers' attention and were instinctively interpreted as instances of empathy.

For instance, one judge displayed an uncanny ability to discern the state of mind and emotional dynamics of an elderly person accused of a petty crime (see also Stępień 2021). This judge then conducted the proceedings with delicate adjustments to accommodate the accused, perfectly recognizing his emotional states and reacting appropriately by sharing some relaxing stories to manage his stress. On another occasion, a different judge reassured a victim with genuine kindness, sincerely assuring them that everything would be all right (and this was not a mere platitude). The judge directed a "human face" to the witness with real concern. In another case, the judge and the official preparing the minutes reacted emotionally upon hearing about the dramatic living conditions of one of the participants in the hearing. Momentarily, the keyboard fell silent, and the judge's face displayed something that could be interpreted as compassion or concern.

These examples highlight the multifaceted nature of judicial behaviors and responses within the courtroom. The first instance can be interpreted as a demonstration of mature empathy, showcasing a profound understanding of the accused's emotional state and needs. The second instance reflects a genuine empathic reaction, where the judge displays understanding and empathy toward the victim, offering more than just superficial reassurance. In the third case, while not strictly empathy, it reveals compassionate and concerned behavior. This diversity emphasizes that judges' reactions during court hearings are nuanced and can encompass various aspects of empathy and distinct processes. These kinds of judicial behavior encountered in courtrooms, in stark contrast to the generally expected "stone face" judicial demeanor ideal in Poland, served as the initial inspiration for further contemplating the actual role of empathy in judicial decision-making. This inspiration arose against the backdrop of a complete lack of discussion about the connections between the act of judging and the experiencing of empathy (not to mention compassion, sympathy, and kindness) within legal education in Poland.

A glimpse into the status quo

As signaled thus far, despite ongoing discussions about various juridical topics, the issue at hand has, surprisingly, not received significant and broad attention. This is particularly intriguing given that empathy is one of the most widely discussed subjects across numerous fields, not only in areas where it has been studied for decades—such as psychology, psychiatry, philosophy, sociology, and, more recently, primatology and neuroscience—but also in fields like leadership studies, pedagogy, and even computer and design studies (see, e.g., Koskinen 2023). Empathy is increasingly recognized as an important, if not the most important, factor contributing to overall well-being. It is seen both as a general resource or "social glue" that enables humans to lead meaningful lives (empathy as a humanistic ideal) and as a tool for better designing solutions with the "user's perspective" in mind (empathy as a tool). This shows that empathy is not only linked to social morality but also plays a role in discussions about efficiency.

The lack of comprehensive studies on empathy within the legal sciences is particularly striking when compared to a significant interest within the medical sciences. The latter field has seen extensive research and empirical studies on the role of empathy, with hundreds of works dedicated to the subject, such as those by Jodi Halpern (2001) and Jean Decety (2020). In various medical professions, the role of empathy is a hotly debated issue. Some argue that empathy enhances medical outcomes in patients and positively impacts the well-being of personnel by reducing occupational burnout. Conversely, others point to the potential drawbacks of empathy, such as the risk of emotional overload or the possibility of distancing healthcare professionals from objective, standard-based measures. Despite continuing debates, empathy is thoroughly researched and systematically taught as a competency for medical professionals.

Against the broader background of law and empathy, a critical review of the current research pertaining to the judicial context should not be misconstrued as suggesting that numerous authors from diverse backgrounds and traditions have not already been exploring this. Chapter 1 of this book is dedicated to presenting and summarizing canonical works on empathy and law, with a particular focus on the role of the former in judicial decision-making. However, it is generally observed that most studies addressing that role primarily pertain to the common law jurisdictions (see, e.g., Henderson 1987; Bandes 1996; Booth 2019; Roach Anleu, Mack 2017, 2021a). This emphasis can be attributed to various factors (including the structural and cultural), as common law jurisdictions often provide more room for application of skills in judging and frequently explore alternatives to formalistic decision-making.

A notable exception comes from Sweden (see, e.g., Bergman Blix, Wettergren 2016; Bergman Blix, Wettergren 2018: 11–12, 107–109, 119, 144, 166), where the role of empathy in the judicial profession and courtrooms has been examined through the lens of law and emotions. Swedish studies focus on the interactional context in which empathy is employed, marking a significant shift from traditional approaches that have mostly concentrated on empathy's impact on judicial decisions.

Explorations of empathy's role in judicial decision-making have adopted various lenses, recognizing the diversity of actors and viewpoints involved. These approaches, however, have often overlooked the thoughts and experiences of justices regarding empathy in their work. Surprisingly, study of this matter has been marginalized for decades, obscuring the challenges, issues, and dilemmas judges face when using empathy in their work. It should be noted that when giving judges a platform to express their views, it is crucial to recognize the specific language they use to conceptualize their work, both for themselves and a broader audience. Judges may be "speaking prose," meaning that—due to fundamental caution in emphasizing the positive relationship between empathy and the law (especially in judging)—they might engage in empathetic practices without explicitly labeling them as such. Without striving to understand their true thoughts (rather than just labeling their actions), it is impossible to fully grasp how judges perceive the role empathy plays in their decision-making.

The importance of judges' perspective

Before presenting the framework underlying this book, it is important to justify the exploration of how social actors—in this case, judges—perceive and understand concepts and terms related to the practices in which they are immersed. Why should we concern ourselves with how judges perceive empathy in their work? Would it not suffice to rely solely on the "objective" understanding of empathy derived from scientific literature when investigating a particular domain, such as the judicial context?

First, the literature dedicated to unraveling the intricate meaning of empathy is remarkably extensive, with numerous books and articles grappling with the inherent vagueness of the concept (see Cuff et al. 2016; Guthridge, Giummarra 2021). This ambiguity serves as both attraction and frustration. On the one hand, it invites broad research and exploration, fostering a wealth of perspectives. On the other hand, the elusive nature of empathy can be a source of irritation, particularly when attempting to pin down a precise definition. Given that no commonly accepted definition of empathy exists, it would be misguided to impose a specific one and then confront judges with it. Furthermore, unconvincing would be some "objective" understanding of empathy equated with what social actors actually associate with the term. Moreover, empathy is often confused with emotions such as sympathy, compassion, pity, or concern. Although the literature frequently distinguishes between these concepts, it is presumptuous to assume that actors do likewise: their blunders in this respect do matter.

Second, even beyond the claim raised earlier, it is important to establish a) how actors understand a given term that is significant in social life, b) to what extent they perceive certain issues associated with it, and c) how they link it (or not) with others. It can be surmised that how judges understand empathy influences their approach to its application in a judicial context or even just impacts how they think about its utility.

Third, when considering innovative judiciary reforms (the broader setting of the considerations presented in this book), the focus should be on the real social and psychosocial processes that impact the delivery and administration of justice, rather than solely on names and labels. This is because we need to understand the actual meanings that actors—i.e., the judges—associate with certain terminology. Only by comparing these actors' perspectives with other data sources or viewpoints can we fully understand a given issue. Judicial empathy raises several arguments for and against its use, but it cannot be fully and fairly addressed without incorporating the perspectives of judges themselves. As deeply involved actors, they have unique and sometimes exclusive access to certain phenomena.

Fourth, it can be assumed that judges' understanding of empathy is influenced by the specific organizational conditions of their work and the requirements of professional culture. As humans, they are shaped by long-term socialization forces—driven by imperatives of standardization, objectification, and the need for neutrality—which strongly influence their ways of thinking. Some professional ideals may appear to conflict with what is typically associated with empathy, but the opposite is also possible. Therefore, focusing on the views and opinions of justices is crucial in assessing the impact of their profession. Understanding how judges perceive issues related to empathy, even beyond the judicial context, provides insights into the structures that shape their thinking and worldview.

Recapping from a social sciences perspective, it is clear that access to internalized conceptualizations is necessary to fully grasp this fragment of the social realm under investigation. Vast traditions such as anthropology, phenomenology, and symbolic interactionism argue for the importance of entering the *emic* perspective—the viewpoint of the participants themselves. However, legal sciences, through an objectivizing lens, typically focus on defining concepts, distinguishing between them, and clarifying meanings, but this often marginalizes what legal actors have conceptualized for themselves. The considerations noted earlier call for transcending this habit within the legal disciplines—to underscore the comprehension of personal worlds, particularly with respect to how judges understand empathy and its role in their work.

Research framework and the research questions

In response to two key calls—to broaden the scope of empathy studies in judicial decision-making beyond common law jurisdictions and to investigate judges' viewpoints on the role of empathy in their work—the research underpinning this volume explores the opinions and experiences of Polish judges regarding empathy in judicial decision-making. By prioritizing their perspectives, a more comprehensive exploration of this issue is achieved.

Before outlining the specific research questions, it is important to clarify the general research framework that has guided the study. This is crucial because although the study focuses on Polish judges, some arguments and theoretical findings extend beyond these parameters. An objective is to cast a widespread light on ideas about empathy's place in the judicial work, viewing this issue as embedded within the discourse on how to reform the judiciary.

The initial premise of this study is that nearly all humans possess rudimentary levels of empathy. Setting aside intricate definitions, empathy can be understood as the capacity to open up one's perspective by stepping into someone else's shoes—for one person to resonate with the emotions, thoughts, standpoints, and situation of another. In essence, the ability to grasp these facets of the other is crucial for any social being, including judges. Therefore, judges, as human beings, are assumed to be capable of empathy—the donning of a robe does not erase inherent capabilities. However, this does not preclude individual variations and idiosyncrasies in empathetic abilities. The central question then becomes: What happens to empathy during a judge's career, given that hard-wired inclinations cannot be entirely expunged or suspended?

This line of thinking encourages us to consider the social conditions that influence both the long-term empathetic work that takes place over a judge's professional lifetime and the actual application of empathy under specific circumstances. This approach challenges the conventional view of empathy as a process merely mental, permitting something akin to "mental teleportation." In fact, certain social contexts or professional settings may foster the cultivation of empathetic competencies, as is often the case in caregiving vocations. Conversely, other environments may inhibit empathy or discourage its expression, sometimes even exerting pressure to curtail its use. Arlie Hochschild (2013: Chapter 3) introduced the concept of "empathic maps"—socially and culturally regulated guidelines on where and how strongly to be open and express such impulses. These maps dictate with whom to empathize or not. Hochschild also introduced the term "empathic walls"—socially constructed and individually negotiated barriers against delving deeply into another person. In some sense, structured occupational environments provide or induce "empathic maps and walls." Building on these concepts, Natalia Ruiz-Junco (2017) proposed an analytical framework for the sociology of empathy, based on the assumption that we need to consider how the external social environment interacts with the internal mental states typically associated with empathy. She presented concepts such as empathy frames, empathy rules, empathy performances, and empathy paths. This sociological perspective on empathy provides a strong foundation for the approach presented in this book. Expanding on this perspective, we can highlight and track the long-term processes that model people's empathic dispositions within their cultural and work environments.

Hochschild's (1983) earlier elaborated notion of "emotional labor"—the managing of one's emotions in response to organizational and economic forces over time—has been successfully applied to judges and their work milieux (see Wojciechowski et al. 2015; Roach Anleu, Mack 2021a, 2021b; Snider et al. 2022; Barry et al. 2023). Building on that, Hochschild also introduced the concept of "empathy labor." This concept explores how structured social settings influence and shape individuals' empathetic skills. These capacities can be muted, marginalized, or, conversely, developed and integrated as a social role demands. Unlike Jamil Zaki's concept of "motivated empathy" (2014; see Cameron 2018), which focuses on the situational activation of empathy, empathy labor refers to the enduring, continuous, and often tacit process of molding the empathetic potential and dispositions of justices.

The judicial profession is undoubtedly unique and distinctive, providing an exceptionally structured environment for that empathy labor. The work of judges is regulated by a multitude of legal and organizational norms, including both abstract and concrete elements. Courtrooms and court sites possess idiosyncratic architectural and spatial characteristics that create an inimitable atmosphere. Courts also develop their own organizational cultures, shaped by the traditions and norms of the legal profession. The primary task of judges—coming to a decision and providing justifications—often requires them to conceal their own dispositions, thoughts, and personal appraisals. Despite differences in judicial conduct across diverse jurisdictions, it is generally thought that judges should occlude their personal thoughts and feelings. Normative and cultural factors, as well as the inherent features of third-party dispute resolution, necessitate an outer shell of impartiality and neutrality. Judges, while afforded some autonomy in their empathy labor, work within environments similarly structured and shaped by long-standing occupational acculturation.

In the Polish legal system, the career trajectory of judges follows a civil service model (see a more detailed description in Chapter 2). Young individuals undergo extensive specialized training, typically lasting a minimum of ten years (including an MA in law), before becoming judges. Their careers are heavily dependent on periodic evaluations of their work and decisions by specific bodies. Consequently, their professional choices and even their personalities are significantly influenced by the bureaucratic logic associated with hierarchical court structures and strategic decision-making (see Epstein, Weinshall 2021). The prevailing professional culture emphasizes a stone-faced judicial demeanor as ideal (Wojciechowski et al. 2015). Socialization into the judicial role is a lengthy, incessant process.

Nonetheless, despite the aims and strength of that socialization, it is important to remember, as Jerome Frank poignantly noted (1931), that judges—Polish judges included—are human beings. Judges naturally possess capabilities that are not confined solely to their professional roles but are also triggered by and expressed in their private lives. Hence, just as they are expected to cooperate and attune with others in personal relationships, glimpses of empathy are discernible within Polish courtrooms (as discussed in Stępień 2021). Despite a general lack of awareness or discussion within the legal community, judicial empathy seems quite present in the courtroom, albeit sitting discreetly and unrecognized as such.

To sum up the Polish context, certain factors (such as the nature of the judicial role and the features of the professional culture) initially seem to marginalize the role of empathy in judging or even discredit its possibility. On the other hand, empathetic skills seem indispensable in certain types of cases, such as those in family courts or in specific scenarios where a judge's empathetic engagement is warranted. There is space for various processes driven by ideals of procedural justice or the therapeutic impact of courts and judges and a humanistic appeal that collectively emphasizes the need for a judge's empathy.

Given these conflicting dynamics, judges find themselves—whether or not they are aware of it—engaged in continual navigation of their empathetic inclinations. This can be described as precisely the empathy labor undertaken by judges and suggests the potential for a clash between professional skepticism toward empathy and the simultaneous need for it in some situations. This leads to a nuanced interplay between officially endorsed anti-empathetic stances (or silence on the issue) and the possibility of unspoken, covert, or intentional empathy. Thus, the core of the investigation here pertains to how judges manage such capacities throughout their careers, specifically within professional milieux. This refers to both conscious and subconscious processes wherein the empathic disposition of a justice is managed by external social forces.

Empathy labor constitutes a prevailing reference point for this book, taking into account the broader processes of judicial socialization and work environments, which significantly shape how judges express their empathetic tendencies in a judicial setting. That said, specific inquiries revolve around the perception among Polish justices of the role actually played by empathy in their work. The study at hand aims to distill the views and experiences of Polish judges regarding this issue, focusing on both descriptive and prescriptive dimensions.

In terms of the descriptive aspect, the main research questions are as follows: How do Polish judges perceive the role of empathy in their work, and what are their experiences in this regard? On the prescriptive side, the research questions explore what Polish judges perceive as a desirable level of empathy in their work. This distinction assumes obstacles and barriers to employing empathy—if they view it positively—or reasons to limit its use in the judicial sphere—if they view it negatively. The study aims to map different opinions and experiences related to empathy as recounted by a diverse set of Polish judges (hereafter simply referred to as "judges").

Designing the research to dig deeper, we focused on detailed issues and posed specific research questions:

- How do judges understand empathy, and what do they think of certain of its characteristics, such as its relation to compassion and morality?
- Where do judges see points in the decision-making process in which empathy is or cannot be applied?
- In the judicial context, what obstacles to using empathy (when needed or desired) do judges distinguish?
- To what extent are judges aware of potential problems related to the use of empathy in their decision-making?
- Do these judges' views and experiences align with points raised in the literature, particularly concerning the relationship between empathy and impartiality?

Although Chapter 2 discusses the methodology employed in the research, it is important to mention here that, in order to address the previously listed questions, the principal investigators—Ewa Wilczek-Rużyczka and Mateusz Stępień—conducted a series of in-depth interviews with judges, collecting data from 37 participants. In addition, three focus groups were later conducted with family judges, whose views and experiences regarding empathy in their work appeared to differ significantly from the rest of the sample. The decision to adopt a qualitative research approach for this study was based on the belief that intimate conversations with judges would yield valuable insights into their perceptions of their work. However, this methodological choice presented numerous challenges and dilemmas, which are extensively discussed in Chapter 2.

Despite beginning with straightforward research questions about a single jurisdiction, the study's relevance extends beyond the mere presentation of empirical data. Those questions are situated within the realm of empathy labor, a novel concept in the context of the judicial process. This focus aims to stimulate the exploration of far-reaching changes in the personalities, traits, maturation, and, more broadly, development of justices in their social role. This book advocates for a developmental approach to the process of becoming a judge (for a developmental approach to judicial empathy, see Stępień 2025).

The empirical emphasis should not lead to an impression that theoretical contributions (beyond the inherently rich empathy labor concept) are overlooked. We delve here into the putative difference between applying empathy in judicial decision-making and the development of something specific—judicial empathy in general. The latter can be seen as the integration of empathetic abilities with the demands and conditions of the judicial role. The perspectives of Polish judges contribute to further exploration of this possibility. Additionally, the presented findings are compared to existing literature pertaining to other jurisdictions. The book also offers in Chapter 1 a detailed reconstruction of current discussions and research on empathy and law, especially in a judicial context. Finally, the book's last chapter sketches a preliminary structure for empathy training for judges. These aspects mean that this volume can be of practical use beyond studies of the Polish judiciary: It could facilitate the distinction of more practice-oriented training solutions.

Synopsis

To briefly present the structure and essence of the content, the first chapter, entitled "Empathy in the Legal Context: Advances and Gaps in Current Research," provides a summary of and commentary on contemporary studies concerning empathy and law, particularly in the context of judicial decision-making. This chapter offers a short overview of various philosophical threads, including sentimentalism, the ethics of care, and feminism. It further explores established intellectual movements (such as therapeutic jurisprudence as well as the law and emotions movement), all of which investigate the relationships between empathy and the law. The primary goal of the chapter is to understand how empathy is conceptualized within the studies on the legal domain. The chapter also includes an extended discussion on empirical research regarding the role of empathy in judicial decision-making. Special weight is placed on studies that seek to explore how judges perceive empathy within their professional roles. Due to the limited number of studies specifically examining this aspect, the chapter thoroughly reviews the existing literature in order to reconstruct relevant points as articulated by justices from various jurisdictions.

The second chapter, "Methodology, Study Context, and Challenges," plays a pivotal role in framing and contextualizing the study. It offers readers insights into the ongoing legal and constitutional crisis in Poland, with a specific focus on the period from 2021 to 2022 when the research was conducted. This contextual information is crucial as it sets the stage and helps readers understand the social and political backdrop of the study. Additionally, the chapter provides a comprehensive overview of the organization and structure of the Polish judicial system, shedding light on the nature of judicial training. This information is particularly valuable for readers who may not be familiar with this system, laying a solid foundation for comprehension of the environment in which the judges under study operate. Presented, too, is elucidation of the applied methodology. Furthermore, acknowledgement of the methodological challenges encountered during the research itself lends transparency to the study and highlights the complexities involved when extracting a judge's experiences and perspectives on empathy labor. Finally, the chapter offers additional insight into the sample of justices in Poland who participated in the research. That information provides clarity about the scope of the study and key characteristics of the participants.

The third chapter ("Judges and the Struggle to Understand Empathy") tackles a challenging subject: comprehension of how Polish judges perceive empathy. This is a complex topic due to the general ambiguities surrounding the very notion of empathy, not to mention the potential limitations and biases associated with its use in the context of judging. To address this, the researchers asked judges about their initial intuitions and posed specific questions related to activities associated with empathy. This approach allowed for the identification of various clusters of meanings that judges associate with empathy. Chapter 3 not only categorizes those meanings and offers a more nuanced view of how Polish judges understand this concept, but it also compares their viewpoints with the dominant approaches to empathy found in the literature to date. Additionally, the chapter explores how judges see the relations between empathy and morality, empathy and compassion, and their views on the nature of empathy. By going beyond simple and basic questions with regard to these facets, the chapter ultimately offers a comprehensive understanding of how judges think about empathy.

Chapter 4, entitled "Excavating the Role and Place of Empathy in Judicial Decision-Making: The Judge's Perspective," primarily focuses on how Polish judges perceive the role of empathy in their work, acknowledging its presence and significance. The chapter extensively discusses the obstacles judges face when trying to use empathy. The third part of the chapter reconstructs judges' views on the normative question of whether, and for what reasons, judges should or should not be empathetic. This section ponders the professional environs in which judges operate and the significant processes of socialization that shape their roles. Additionally, the chapter proffers preliminary thoughts about how judges perceive changes in their empathetic responses over time.

The fifth chapter, "Empathy and Impartiality 'Friends' or 'Foes'?" dives into how Polish justices perceive the relationship between the application of empathy in the course of their professional work and the concept of impartiality therein. This aspect is discussed in relation to the current literature on empathy, emotions, and impartiality; references are also made to studies that directly explore the empathy-impartiality duo.

The sixth chapter ("Developing Judicial Empathy Through Training Methods: A Psychological Perspective") begins by presenting an all-embracing overview of the origins, determinants, and significance of empathy, as well as the methods used to measure it. The chapter then addresses the training needs of judges, justifying this aspect based on insights gathered during the interviews. The core of this section of the volume outlines an empathetic training system tailored for judges and designed to transcend the idiosyncrasies of specific juridical environments. That system also offers a guide that can be applied and adapted for different groups of judges. The proposed training scenario has been developed on the basis of our dataset in addition to extensive knowledge drawn from empathy training programs for the medical professions.

Finally, the Conclusion provides an overarching review of the experiences and thoughts of Polish judges on empathy-related themes, comparing them to insights gained from judges in other jurisdictions. This section briefly summarizes the answers to the research questions and highlights some more general findings. The closing chapter serves as the culmination of the research, synthesizing its findings and their broader implications.

References

Ames, Roger T. 2022. "恕 *shu*. 'Putting Oneself in the Other's Place, Deference, Empathy, Dramatic Rehearsal'." In *A Conceptual Lexicon for Classical Confucian Philosophy*, edited by Roger T. Ames. 248–257. New York: SUNY Press.

Bandes, Susan A. 1996. "Empathy, Narrative, and Victim Impact Statements." *University of Chicago Law Review* 63: 361–412.

Bandes, Susan A. 2011. "Moral Imagination in Judging." *Washburn Law Review* 51: 1–24.

Barry C. et al. 2023. "The Emotional Labour of Judges in Jury Trials." *Journal of Law and Society* 50: 477–499.

Bergman Blix, Stina and Åsa Wettergren. 2016. "Empathy and Objectivity in the Legal Process: The Case of Swedish Prosecutors." *Journal of Scandinavian Studies in Criminology and Crime Prevention* 17: 19–35.

Bergman Blix, Stina and Åsa Wettergren. 2018. *Professional Emotions in Court: A Sociological Perspective*. London and New York: Routledge.

Booth, Tracey. 2019. "Family Violence and Judicial Empathy: Managing Personal Cross Examination in Australian Family Law Proceedings." *Oñati Socio-Legal Series* 9(5): 702–725.

Cameron, C. Daryl. 2018. "Motivating Empathy: Three Methodological Recommendations for Mapping Empathy." *Social and Personality Psychology Compass* 12: e12418 https://doi.org/10.1111/spc3.12418

Cuff, Benjamin et al. 2016. "Empathy: A Review of the Concept." *Emotion Review* 8(2): 144–153.

Decety, Jean. 2020. "Empathy in Medicine: What It Is, and How Much We Really Need It." *American Journal of Medicine* 133(5): 561–566. https://doi.org/10.1016/j.amjmed.2019.12.012

Dudek, Michał and Mateusz Stępień. 2021. *Power Distance Courtroom Dynamics*. Cham: Springer.

Epstein, Lee and Keren Weinshall. 2021. *The Strategic Analysis of Judicial Behavior: A Comparative Perspective*. Cambridge, MA: Cambridge University Press.

Frank, Jerome. 1930. *Law and the Moder Mind*. New York: Brentano's.

Frank, Jerome. 1931. "Are Judges Human? Part 1: The Effect on Legal Thinking of the Assumption That Judges Behave Like Human Beings." *University of Pennsylvania Law Review* 80: 17–53.

Guthridge, Michaela and Melita Giummarra. 2021. "The Taxonomy of Empathy: A Meta-Definition and the Nine Dimensions of the Empathic System." *Journal of Humanistic Psychology*: 1–25.

Halpern, Jodi. 2001. *From Detached Concern to Empathy: Humanizing Medical Practice*. Oxford: Oxford University Press.

Henderson, Lynne. 1987. "Legality and Empathy." *Michigan Law Review* 85(6): 1574–1653.

Hochschild, Arlie. 1983. *The Managed Heart: Commercialization of Human Feeling*. Berkley: University of California Press.

Hochschild, Arlie. 2013. *So How's the Family and Other Essays*. Berkeley: University of California Press.

Hoffman, Martin L. 2000. *Empathy and Moral Development: Implications for Caring and Justice*. Cambridge: Cambridge University Press.

Koskinen, Llpo. 2023. *Design, Empathy, Interpretation: Toward Interpretive Design*. Cambridge, MA: MIT Press.

Lanzoni, Susan. 2018. *Empathy: A History*. New Haven, CT and London: Yale University Press.
Massaro, Toni M. 1989. "Empathy, Legal Storytelling, and the Rule of Law: New Words, Old Wounds?" *Michigan Law Review* 87: 2099–2127.
Mathis, Klaus and Fabian Diriwächter. 2012. "Is the Rationality of Judicial Judgements Jeopardized by Cognitive Biases and Empathy?" In *Efficiency, Sustainability, and Justice to Future Generations*, edited by Klaus Mathis. 55–73. Cham: Springer.
Roach Anleu, Sharyn and Kathy Mack. 2017. *Performing Judicial Authority in the Lower Courts*. London: Palgrave Macmillan.
Roach Anleu, Sharyn and Kathy Mack. 2021a. *Judging and Emotion A Socio-Legal Analysis*. London: Routledge.
Roach Anleu, Sharyn and Kathy Mack. 2021b. "Emotion Work as Judicial Work." In: *The Judge, the Judiciary and the Court: Individual, Collegial and Institutional Judicial Dynamics in Australia*, edited by G. Appleby and A. Lynch. 143–162. Cambridge: Cambridge University Press.
Ruiz-Junco, Natalia. 2017. "Advancing the Sociology of Empathy: A Proposal." *Symbolic Interaction* 40: 414–435.
Snider Katie M. et al. 2022. "Judges' Emotion: An Application of the Emotion Regulation Process Model." *Psychiatry, Psychology and Law* 29(2): 256–273.
Solum, Lawrence. 2003. "Virtue Jurisprudence: A Virtue-Centered Theory of Judging." *Metaphilosophy* 34: 178–203.
Stępień, Mateusz. 2021. "On the Relationship between Judicial Empathy and the Integrity of Judges." *Krytyka Prawa. Niezależne Studia Nad Prawem* 13(3): 98–113.
Stępień, Mateusz. 2025. "A Developmental Approach to Judicial Empathy." In *Judicial Character in Hard Times: On the Role of Judicial Virtues in Defending the Rule of Law*, edited by Tomasz Widłak. 105–125. London: Edward Elgar.
Wojciechowski, Maciej et al. 2015. "Emotional Labour of Judges." *Archiwum Filozofii Prawa i Filozofii Społecznej* 1(10): 97–110.
Zaki, Jamil. 2014. "Empathy: A Motivated Account." *Psychological Bulletin* 140(6): 1608–1647. https://doi.org/10.1037/a0037679

1 Empathy in the legal context

Advances and gaps in current research

Mateusz Stępień

Introduction

This chapter aims to map the landscape of how empathy and law have been approached in the literature, naturally emphasizing empirical research into empathy's place in the courtroom. Oddly enough, such a review has not been undertaken heretofore; hence we seek to synthesize various approaches and findings, while also highlighting existing gaps. By considering the main typologies of studies in this field, as well as presenting examples of studies that look through the eyes of justices themselves, new vistas will emerge. Indeed, a common and significant omission in the literature is precisely the judges' point of view. That notwithstanding, some studies have striven to capture judges' approaches to empathy, providing supplementary information and integrating personal reflections on empathy. This chapter accentuates such investigations which have enriched the discussion, contributed to a more nuanced and holistic understanding, and, most importantly, provided the underpinning for our research.

Overview of approaches to studying empathy and law

The relationship between empathy and law, while not traditionally a core focus in either the legal sciences or other fields, has generated an array of discussions and studies across a variety of disciplines. In effecting a survey of the current state of scholarship on empathy and law, it is useful to have a categorization of the existing literature.

Between speculative and empirical approaches

One categorization lies in the speculative vis-à-vis empirical approach. Important to note at the start, however, is that the distinction made between them primarily serves presentation purposes. In fact, many studies integrate theoretical frameworks with empirical testing (e.g., expanded application of theories, such as emotion regulation, to courtroom interactions). Additionally, speculative studies are often substantiated by empirical data which is cited and incorporated into an argument.

DOI: 10.4324/9781003546580-2

Speculative studies, a vast and diverse set, often emerge from philosophically oriented works. It is therefore no surprise that studies also explore the connections between empathy and law against the backdrop of themes like justice or the foundations of law. More traditional legal scholars have theorized, too, about the role empathy plays in various spheres of law. Scholars frequently examine empathy through lenses such as impartiality and neutrality, more objectively considering how empathy might align with or challenge these legal principles.

Philosophically oriented works that are quite pertinent to the topic at hand and therefore should be acknowledged include the contributions (as well as modern interpretations) of classic Western thinkers like David Hume and Adam Smith. These philosophers presented comprehensive views of human and social life—implicitly including what we now describe as empathy in their philosophies of law. The foundation provided by Hume and Smith continues to serve as the bedrock of legal philosophy, influencing our modern understandings of the law.

For example, Michel Slote, grounded in Humean sentimentalism and an ethics of care, strongly emphasized empathy's role within the legal sphere. In his opinion, empathy serves as the moral cornerstone of the legal system. He asserts that "empathy and empathic concern for others can function as the (entire) basis for a plausible understanding of legal and social justice" (2013: 287). Importantly, for Slote, the expression of empathic concern is vital to the legitimacy of the legal system. Drawing inspiration from Adam Smith, Martha Nussbaum—another key figure at the intersection of law and empathy—has also emphasized the concept of empathy in legal thinking. Nussbaum argues that Smith's concept of public rationality—based on filtered, nurtured, and augmented sentiments—provides a framework for contemplating the role played by not only empathy but also sympathy and compassion. She asserts that judges must have "the power of imagining vividly what it is like to be each of the persons whose situations he imagines" (1996: 26–27). Nussbaum has long advocated the integration of empathy, as well as related concepts such as imagination, emotions, and literary sensibilities, into standard legal thinking. In her book *Political Emotions*, she rejects the "romantic idea that emotion is not worthy unless it comes unbidden" and urges the use of government rhetoric, public art, and other state-sponsored activities to foster a civic culture of "enhanced empathy" (2013: 65, 381–386). For Nussbaum, this kind of empathy is a crucial public value. All in all, these two examples—Slote's philosophical framing and Nussbaum's application of empathy in public contexts—illustrate that classic philosophical ideas continue to act as significant stimuli that shape our contemporary understanding of the empathy-law relationship.

Along a similar vein of philosophical analysis, Lawrence Hoffman, an icon in the field of empathy studies, has recognized the significance of empathy in the context of law (2011). He positions empathic reactions at the heart of his discussion, as they serve as the moral foundation for the legal system. Stressing that empathy can evoke emotions (such as a profound sense of injustice), he illustrates how it impacts the individuals responsible for initiating legal changes and contributes to the shaping and reforming of laws. Hoffman highlights areas wherein empathy can act as a positive force, but notes that it also possesses biases that can limit its value and utility with regard to a legal situation. In his analysis of judicial opinions, specifically through the work of Lynne Henderson (1987), he contends that some decisions can be categorized as empathetic in the sense that the majority of the decision-makers were "emotionally motivated." This underscores the profound role played by empathy in shaping legal outcomes.

Generally speaking, empirical studies are more prevalent in fields such as criminology, the sociology of law, and various branches of social sciences that study law (mostly social psychology). These studies frequently employ experimental or quasi-experimental methodologies, such as mock juries or judges, to examine how empathy—whether as a situationally induced response, temporary state of mind, or stable trait—prompts legal decision-making, particularly in determining guilt or sentencing (e.g., Johnson et al. 2002; Cormack 2021; see also Wood et al. 2014). Notably, when empathy is operationalized as something closer to "easy empathy"—an automatic and uncontrollable response (see Chapter 3)—judges' experiences seem to be a factor that has led to biased decisions. However, such a tendency also informs discussions on court diversity and court packing. Additionally, observational and interview techniques are increasingly being used to evaluate how empathy functions with judicial settings (e.g., Bergman Blix, Wettergren 2018; Barry et al. 2023), where legal professionals may express and utilize empathy for various purposes. These studies are often concentrated on specific aspects of the legal system—such as a single type of decision or a particular type of empathy considered at a specific time and place. An abundance of cases—some of which are presented next—demonstrate how empirical approaches can be applied to the topic at hand.

Empathy as a core or just an element of the interest

Empathy literature relevant to the legal field can be further categorized based on its part in the overall argument: works in which empathy is peripheral and those in which it is central. The former—with empathy discussed within broader domains such as law and emotions, justice, biases, or judicial decision-making—is more prevalent; the latter is more rare, although a direct focus in empirical studies and analyses is not unknown. Still, while looking at empathy, authors tend to concentrate on a single aspect (e.g., the role of empathy in sentencing). In contrast, the volume at hand is among the earliest efforts to place empathy at the center of scholarly attention.

At times, empathy merely figures on a list of desirable judicial traits. For example, Richard A. Posner (2008: 117) identified it as a component of "good judgment," describing it as "an elusive faculty best understood as a compound of empathy, modesty, maturity, a sense of proportion, balance, recognition of human limitations, sanity, prudence, a sense of reality, and common sense."

This is, in fact, a typical example of an episodic reference, although empathy plays a role disproportionately more profound. Interestingly, empathy has been a consistent topic of discussion within certain well-established intellectual movements in academia, such as feminism, therapeutic jurisprudence, and law and emotion. Empathy in studies arising out of these movements deserves further explication.

The feminist approach, noticeably diverse and pluralistic, has explored empathy in law extensively. Feminist jurisprudence has emphasized a need for empathy as a general tool (one among many) by way of shifting the orientation of the law. Rosemary Hunter acknowledged retrospectively that some feminist thinkers have argued that values traditionally associated with the private sphere (e.g., care, connection, and empathy) should be extended into the public—including the legal realm (2013: 21). This approach envisions greater empathy, reorienting the law toward novel sets of values and altering how it operates. In the 1980s, the ethics of care (developed within feminist frameworks, notably by Carol Gilligan) played the most critical role in a shift that energized feminist thought. This led to the introduction of empathy—along with compassion and a favoring of judicial compassion (see Colker 1989)—into these discussions.

Another movement arising in American academia that has impacted studies of empathy and law is therapeutic jurisprudence. Authors associated with this practically oriented philosophy of law also emphasize strongly a need for empathy in the legal domain. This approach centers on enhancement of the therapeutic aspects of the legal system; in doing so, it, too, advocates a reorientation of the traditional goals of the law. With a primary focus on the judicial realm, therapeutic jurisprudence highlights the importance of empathy when conducting reforms of legal institutions and principles. Its proponents provide a framework for institutional reforms, including the introduction of problem-solving courts, and also redefine the preferred model of judging and the qualities of a good judge. From this perspective, empathy is considered key in bringing about coveted change (see Rużyczka 2023). For instance, Bruce J. Winick, one of the movement's founders, lists a range of qualities that judges should possess to achieve therapeutic goals. These qualities include "warmth, openness, emotional attachment, empathy, respect, active listening, a positive focus, non-coercion, non-paternalism, clarity, and plain language" (Winick 2002–2003: 1068). Therapeutic jurisprudence argues for replacing "the formalistic, adversarial, and distant judicial role with a more active, involved, collaborative, and less formal administration that demonstrates judicial care and empathy" (Perlman 2018: 70). Importantly, Winick emphasizes that affective empathy is also important: "the judge should convey both an intellectual response to the individual, communicating that she understands the individual's predicament, and an emotional response, communicating that she shares the individual's feelings" (2003–2003: 1069). Such a declaration represents an argument not often made for cognitive, but rather affective empathy.

The third and final movement we explore here is that of law and emotion (see Maroney 2011; Bandes et al. 2021), which also put empathy on the radar. As in the previously mentioned examples, here, too, the study of empathy in the legal, mostly judicial, sphere is a small piece of a larger agenda: the objective is to unveil the role emotions, feelings, and affects play in the functioning of the law and to ask why that role is marginalized in the legal setting. Of course, internal trends are diversified; hence the movement functions as an umbrella. Within the movement one can pinpoint a strong thread of emotion regulation theory being applied to the judicial sphere. For example, emotions that are "backgrounded and subconscious" might motivate judges to avoid empathy (Wettergren, Bergman Blix 2016: 43), but judges do use empathy in their interactions with others. Describing it as a "crucial tool" in emotion management, Bergman Blix and Wettergren point to situations where judges have employed empathy, such as when they assess their "appearance of impartiality from the perspective of the defendant" (2016: 35).

In lieu of our commentary on the ways empathy has been studied within the law and emotion movement (or to discuss crucial findings and obstacles), we look to Susan Bandes, an undeniably pivotal figure in the field. Her take challenges the traditional marginalization of emotions in the legal realm and legal academia, but without necessarily advocating for unrestricted use. Thus, her work does not imply an unqualified endorsement of integrating emotions into legal practice. Instead, Bandes argues for a nuanced understanding of the actual role that emotions (including empathy) play in law, while cautioning against an uncritical elevation of their importance (what she refers to as "the dark underbelly of empathy").

In her foundational paper (1996; see Pemberton 2016), Bandes critically examines victim impact statements (VISs)—the narratives presented by victims and/or family members during the sentencing phase of criminal trials in order to give voice to the emotional impact of a crime. Bandes argues that while VISs are powerful, they introduce emotions that may be inappropriate during sentencing. Specifically, she warns that VISs can evoke empathy toward the victim, but at the cost of degrading the perpetrator. This, she contends, can lead to a form of emotional bias that undermines the fairness and impartiality of the sentencing process. Bandes (1996: 393) argues that such emotional narratives should be suppressed rather than supported, as they introduce an imbalance that distorts the justice process:

> victim impact statements illustrate the pitfalls of acontextually prioritizing any emotion—no matter how benign the emotion may seem. Likewise, they illustrate that storytelling can be used for distinctly unprogressive ends. Ultimately, they illustrate the emptiness of the concepts of empathy and narrative when they are not constrained by extrinsic normative, political, or moral principles.

Bandes expanded upon and clarified this argument in her later work (2009, see also 2011), in which she discussed empathy as a tool that judges can either use appropriately under suitable conditions, or misapply, leading to unjust outcomes. She contended (2009: 136) that empathy cannot be treated simply as an emotion, stating that:

> empathy is a capacity, not an emotion. It differs from sympathy or compassion, both of which are emotions. Empathy entails understanding another person's perspective. Sympathy is a feeling for or with the object of the emotion. Empathy does not require, or necessarily lead to, sympathy. Empathy, unlike sympathy, does not necessarily lead to action on behalf of its object, or the desire to take action on his behalf.

This is an important distinction, as empathy is rightly conceptualized not as an emotion, but as a capacity that is used in contexts wherein emotions play a vivid role. Overall, Bande's work has challenged the marginalization of emotions (as well as related processes such as empathizing) in the legal field. She has cautioned, too, against uncritical use of emotional responses, emphasizing the dangers of selective empathy (discussed later), or the need for careful consideration of how and which emotions are and should be deployed in judicial decision-making.

Summing up, empathy—as part of the feminist, therapeutic jurisprudence, and law and emotions movements—does play a role, albeit not always the main one. Nevertheless, it is framed as an element that contributes to new perspectives for thinking about the law, offering more holistic and human-centered approaches to understanding legal processes and decision-making.

Arguments for or against empathy in law

Much of the controversy in this field hinges upon differing interpretations of what empathy entails and what its role is in the legal process. Unsurprisingly, the debate over empathy in law is marked by both strong backing and equally strong criticism. With respect to the former, numerous works defend its importance, often portraying it as a moral foundation of justice, a humane counterbalance to a perceived legal coldness, and/or a tool by which decision-makers gather relevant information. In these contexts, empathy is sometimes positioned as an alternative to "formalist," "mechanical," or "overly abstract" approaches. Discussions about its role and merits within the judicial field reflect such varied impetuses. For instance, Lynne Henderson, a highly influential author in the field, views empathy as a tool that enables decision makers to "appreciate the human meanings of a given legal situation" (1987: 1576). Similarly, Terry Maroney and Phillip Ackerman-Lieberman highlight the general benefits of empathy, noting that it "widens judges' field of vision and zone of concern" and "expands judges' imaginative universe, tethering their rulings to a factually correct sense of human realities" (2014: 242, 249). On the whole, most works in this category advocate for incorporating empathy into legal practice as a desirable (albeit imperfect) element that should be supplemented by other factors. The literature generally avoids excessive optimism, recognizing that while empathy is valuable, it must be integrated with other considerations to be effective.

With respect to the latter, however, a skeptical or critical stance toward empathy—questioning its utility in the legal realm—dominates popular imaginaries. Brenner Fissell (2016; see also Zipursky 2012) even referred to a "modern anti-empathic consensus." In particular, the use of empathy by judges has provoked some of the most intensive arguments against it. Typical contentions center on its potential to undermine judicial impartiality and objectivity, as well as possibly amplify the subjectivity of decision-makers. Significantly, even proponents of judicial empathy acknowledge some of its limitations. Henderson—though one of the most consistent and prominent supporters—highlighted the existence of empathic biases (1987: 1574–1653):

> the reality of empathy is that we are more likely to empathize with people similar to ourselves, and that such empathic understanding may be so automatic that it goes unnoticed: elites will empathize with the experience of elites, men empathize with men, women with women, whites with whites. I would call this "unreflective" empathy.

Similarly, Bandes (1996) warned against "selective empathy," which occurs when a judge empathizes more easily with and may unconsciously favor a party whose background is similar, as opposed to one with a dissimilar life experience. This empathy bias can lead to unequal treatment in the courtroom and even the rendering of unjust decisions. Bandes rightly argues that judges should be accountable for their own capacity for empathy, its limits, and its "blind spots." Here, empathy, while a neutral tool, can be used to achieve various goals, and its unreflective use can introduce biases.

Empirical research upholds these authors' concerns about selective empathy. Studies have shown a significant empathic divide between judges and defendants in the U.S. criminal justice system, who often differ in terms of race, socioeconomic status, and educational background. This divide can lead judges to allocate empathy unevenly, influencing both their decisions and the perspectives of juries. Scholars such as Craig Haney (2004) and Mona Lynch and Craig Haney (2011) have explored this concept, suggesting that the empathic divide exacerbates biases within the legal system, further entrenching disparities in justice outcomes. In capital punishment cases, Haney (2004) emphasized that generating empathy for the defendant—usually through the presentation of a mitigating narrative during sentencing—is crucial in persuading jurors to choose life over death. She argues that Black defendants, in particular, may be at a disadvantage when faced with predominantly white jurors. Notably, in these scenarios, empathy is something induced in jurors, and the similarity bias associated with empathy leads to differential treatment.

It should be stressed that "unreflexive" or "selective" empathy, which can result in biases during the decision-making process, constitutes but one facet of empathy-related processes. Chapter 3 offers a differentiation between "easy" and "difficult" empathy, where the former provides space for unreflexivity and selectivity, while the latter, paradoxically, facilitates resistance to automatic responses.

Domains of empathy research in law

Empathy is studied in relation to both application of the law and the law-making process. Notably, only a few works have explored the latter from an empathetic perspective (e.g., Posick et al. 2014), while the majority has focused on the judicial context, examining various facets of how empathy interacts with judicial decision-making.

Some investigations have focused on the process by which judges are selected, a topic that gained significant attention following statements by Barack Obama, both as a senator and later as president of the United States. Obama's emphasis on empathy as a crucial quality of judges ignited widespread debate, particularly during and after the Senate hearings for Sonia Sotomayor's nomination to the Supreme Court of the United States. Obama argued that judges who possess empathy should be prioritized in nominations, asserting that empathy is essential for understanding how laws impact the daily realities of people's lives. This position sparked extensive debate over whether empathy is a judicial virtue or vice, with the majority opinion at the time leaning toward the latter.

Although this debate has been widely covered, there remains a need to clarify what Obama, a former professor of constitutional law, actually meant by advocating for empathy in the judiciary. Explaining his criteria for replacing Justice Souter, Obama stated,

> I will seek someone who understands that justice isn't about some abstract legal theory or footnote in a casebook; it is also about how our laws affect the daily realities of people's lives—whether they can make a living and care for their families; whether they feel safe in their homes and welcome in their own nation. I view that quality of empathy, of understanding and identifying with people's hopes and struggles, as an essential ingredient for arriving at just decisions and outcomes.
>
> (Press Briefing by Press Secretary Robert Gibbs)

Obama's remarks highlight two key components of empathy: understanding and identification. While the understanding aspect is generally uncontroversial, the notion of identification—particularly with people's "hopes and struggles"—proved more contentious. This identification refers to the broader socioeconomic conditions and lived experiences of individuals, suggesting that judges should not be isolated from the everyday realities of less fortunate or marginalized people. The emphasis on the colloquial consequences of judicial decisions further underscores Obama's call for judges to avoid a cloistered perspective disconnected from the experiences of ordinary citizens. Obama's statements reinvigorated ongoing debates over empathy's place in the courtroom, revealing that empathy is understood and evaluated differently depending on which aspects are accentuated. This divergence in understanding determines how empathy is assessed in terms of its usefulness and appropriateness in the judicial sphere. The debate highlighted the complexities of incorporating empathy into legal decision-making and underscored the broader implications for legal theory and practice.

Some have emphasized the judicial process itself, highlighting the role of empathy—both positive and negative—in reaching not only final decisions but also other important determinations throughout the trial. Empathy's role in the former is more controversial, while its influence on the latter has not received much attention. Most authors stress the importance of empathy in determining the factual basis of a case, as it allows for a broader understanding of the context. For example, Bandes argues that "a judge uses empathy as a tool towards understanding conflicting claims. Empathy assists the judge in understanding the litigants' perspectives" (2009: 137). Rarely, however, is empathy considered a factor in determining the legal basis of a decision (see Corso 2014 on empathy in the interpretation of constitutional rights).

There has also been research investigating how decision-makers' empathy affects the sentencing process (see Cormack 2021). A substantial body of research, including texts mentioned earlier, have delved into the biases that empathy might activate in judges or jurors. Studies have explored the impact of judicial empathy stemming from a) personal experience (e.g., being a father of daughters) and rulings related to the abuse of women (Glynn, Sen 2015); b) minority group belonging and decisions in employment cases involving civil rights (Weinberg, Nielsen 2012); and c) gender-related empathy and judicial rulings pertaining to sexual discrimination (Moyer, Haire 2015; Roach Anleu, Mack 2021a).

An example of studies that focus on intermediate, yet weighty, decisions is Tracey Booth's body of work (2019) on the factors influencing judges' decisions about protective measures for domestic violence victims in Australia—particularly when victims are cross-examined by an accused representing himself or herself. Booth emphasized the need for judges to fully grasp the position held in the courtroom by both the victim and the perpetrator. She has argued that empathy is crucial to gaining an understanding, but raised questions about when and how empathy is (not) activated by judges in these challenging situations. Booth's analyses have highlighted the role of various sentiments (e.g., fear, anger, and "background emotions") which might cause judges to avoid or minimize an empathic response to a domestic violence victim. Booth employed an emotion regulation framework, combined with a motivated approach to empathy, in order to explore how such emotional dynamics influence judicial decision-making. Booth suggested that empathy can play a dual role in these contexts. On one hand, an empathic response might be directed toward victims, recognizing their emotional experience within the legal process. On the other hand, judges must also consider the perspective of the perpetrators, who may experience negative emotional responses or potential harm to their legal standing if restricted in presenting their case. Despite this dual consideration, Booth critiqued current judicial practices and decisions in Australia, arguing that there has often been a dearth of empathy shown toward these victims, consequently leading to decisions that exacerbated the trauma and distress. Booth's findings suggest that while empathy does not necessarily dictate a specific outcome—such as the automatic imposition of protective measures—it is vital for judges to more deeply explore and understand the victim's situation and perspective. In Booth's view, greater judicial empathy toward victims could lead to more sensitive and protective legal responses that are better aligned with the needs of those who have experienced domestic violence.

A significant body of research, particularly within American academia, has focused on the presence or absence of judicial empathy as evidenced in the judicial opinions themselves. This line of inquiry has generally involved detailed discourse analyses of judicial decisions to identify traces of empathy, explore its role in decision-making, and examine how it is expressed in the justification of rulings. A pioneering study in this field was by Henderson (1987), who analyzed Supreme Court opinions in landmark cases such as *Brown v. Board of Education*, *Shapiro v. Thompson*, *Roe v. Wade*, and *Bowers v. Hardwick*. Henderson pinpointed the presence or absence of empathy in these rulings, highlighting how it influenced both the outcomes of cases and the manner in which decisions were substantiated.

Indeed, it has been common among U.S. scholars to base their theoretical claims on a close reading of judicial opinions, analyzing the narrative structures to track the presence or absence of empathy within the legal reasoning. For example, Thomas Colby (2012), Andrea McArdle (2012), and Rebecca Lee (2014) have all undertaken such analyses, focusing on how empathy is woven into or omitted from judicial narratives and its implications for justice. Megan Pearson (2020) also utilized this approach in her study of empathy and procedural justice in the American legal system, analyzing the narratives arising out of two pivotal discrimination cases (*Masterpiece Cakeshop v. Colorado Civil Rights Commission* and *Lee v. Ashers Baking Company*). Pearson's findings highlighted the crucial role empathy has played in achieving the goals of procedural justice, suggesting that empathy can enhance fairness and legitimacy in judicial processes. Additionally, another noteworthy study by Jennifer Cornell (2022) explored the potential for developing empathy through the reading of judicial opinions. Cornell argued that judicial opinions could be deliberately crafted to foster empathy in their readers, thereby contributing to a more empathetic legal culture.

For years, the management of legal hearings was not a focal point in the study of empathy. However, thanks to the work of Swedish (e.g., Stina Bergman Blix) and Australian (Sharyl Roach Anleu and Kathy Mack) scholars, the law and emotion movement has extended toward areas closely aligned with sociology and the sociology of emotions. Examined by these scholars have been the way judges handle hearings, how legal professionals interact, and how they ensure the well-being of witnesses or defendants—all through the lens of empathy. This area of research has also included studies on virtual hearings and how these settings influence the possibility and expression of empathy (Bandes, Feigenson 2021).

Beyond a distinction between making and applying laws, there have been studies investigating empathy in legal practice: the role of empathy in lawyers' day-to-day work (e.g., Gallacher 2012; Jones 2017); law enforcement, including policing (e.g., Eliasson, DeHart 2023); and the penitentiary context (Lewicka-Zelent, Pytka 2020). Further, a cluster of authors has measured the level of empathy among law students by using a psychometric index (e.g., Spivak et al. 2018; Wilczek-Rużyczka, Kupczyk 2021). Some have speculated about expanding the teaching of and developing empathy in law schools (e.g., Rosenberg 2002; Gascón-Cuenca 2018; Lawton et al. 2022).

Jurisdictions conducive to the study of empathy and law

The existing literature on empathy in law can also be categorized based on jurisdictions in which relevant research has been conducted. Expectedly, studies from common law jurisdictions dominate in this regard. Contemporary discussions began in the United States during the 1980s, propelled by momentum in two of the earlier-described movements as well as a new one: feminist philosophy (second-wave feminism), law and emotion, and, finally here, law and literature. The last of these proposes that empathic abilities are cultivated through fine literature: reading such textual matter expands a capacity for imagination necessary for the enhancement of legal decision-making (Nussbaum 1996; Morawetz 1996; Reichman 2006; Gaakeer 2019). The popularity of critical legal studies, also in the 1980s, sparked further discussions about alternative visions of law and legal decision-making. During this period, U.S.-based academia slowly began incorporating empathy into its broader legal discussions—primarily focusing on the judicial context, but not without addressing the political and ideological implications of its application.

In a sense, it was Henderson who summarized the vibrant discussions around these new threads and provided a comprehensively built claim that empathy does not undermine the rule of law (1987, 1988). This argument should be interpreted as an element in struggles to corroborate how judging is a nonreductive decision-making process: It is inherently loaded with the human factor in which feelings and embodiment play a strong role. This echoed William J. Brennan's (then a highly influential Supreme Court justice) restoration of a demand for the "dimension of passion, of empathy, necessary for a full understanding of the human beings affected by those procedures" (1988: 21). According to Justice Brennan, empathy is attentiveness to the range of human experience as well as a "sensitivity to one's intuitive and passionate responses" (1988: 10). Therefore, judicial empathy takes place when a judge enters the skin of another, making a litigant's experience part of the judge's experience.

In line with this thinking, Henderson importantly asserted that empathy augments both the process of discovery and of justifications, although her inquiries referred to the latter. Hence, she traced judicial opinions displaying signs of empathy (i.e., infused with "the language of empathetic understanding, of feeling the feelings of the people affected by the case," see Henderson [1987: 1574–1653]), as well as those seeming to display none. Henderson is responsible for an excellent discussion of empathy as an "imaginative experiencing of the situation of another" (1987: 1574–1653); she examined its role in Supreme Court jurisprudence as well as in broader legal discourse. Interestingly, Henderson established practices which continue to be the most popular in American legal studies: to trace empathy through analysis of the judicial opinions that are both gateways into decision-making and tools for decision justification. Nevertheless, this introduces another quandary: how to identify a) empathy in consecutive stages of the process leading to a judgement and b) an empathic style in the narrative of judicial opinions.

Naturally, other common law jurisdictions, particularly the UK and Australia, have also merged empathy with both philosophical discussions about law and justice and more focused studies on how empathy influences judicial or juror decisions. The structure of common law systems, with their reliance on ad hoc jurors and adversarial proceedings, forms a distinctive milieu for examining interpersonal interactions in court. In these settings, empathy becomes relevant due to the significant impact that courtroom dynamics, including the emotional atmosphere and participant relations, can have on legal outcomes. Common law jurisdictions open more opportunities for skills-based approaches to judging, and, as a consequence, frequently explore alternatives to formalistic decision-making. These features mean that common law systems are a fertile ground for studies evaluating how empathy operates in legal settings. This, in turn, allows for deeper exploration of how emotional understanding and interpersonal skills contribute to a form of justice outside strict legal reasoning.

There is nevertheless a growing interest in such studies beyond common law jurisdictions, especially in judicial settings. A notable exception to the dominance of common law scholarship is work emerging from the Swedish school (detailed later), led by Stina Bergman Blix. This school of thought combines interactional sociology, particularly Erving Goffman's theories, with emotion regulation frameworks. Offering a valuable counterpoint to the dominant trend, this innovative approach has provided fresh insights into how empathy functions in civil law trials. It has also inspired other European scholars—such as Alessandra Missalle (2023) who studied Italian courts—to explore empathy in different judicial settings. In Poland, for example, exploratory studies have been conducted (Stępień 2021), albeit not directly aligned with the Swedish school. Indeed, the volume at hand builds upon a recognition of the fact that theoretical deliberations and empirical research regarding judicial empathy are crucial in all jurisdictions. Amalgamating here perspectives from diverse legal systems and cultural contexts, we proffer a novel, expanded dataset of judicial experiences and reflections on empathy.

Profound exceptions

Research into empathy's role in judicial decision-making has employed a range of lenses, acknowledging the diversity of actors and viewpoints involved. However, as already discussed in the Introduction, investigations have often overlooked the thoughts and experiences of judges themselves regarding empathy in their work. Surprisingly, this specific, internal perspective has been marginalized for decades, resulting in the unique experiences, challenges, issues, and dilemmas of judges being occluded by generalizations and wishful thinking. Without frank information and true comprehension of their decision-making processes, it is impossible to grasp what role empathy plays in the reaching of a judicial verdict or opinion.

With time, more authors have sought to shed light on judges' perspectives regarding empathy. The methodology and findings of Stina Bergman Blix and her associates are particularly noteworthy. She and others in her circle conducted a series of studies primarily focused on the emotional dimensions of the judicial sphere (Wettergren, Bergman Blix 2016; Bergman Blix, Wettergren 2018; Bergman Blix 2019; Bladini, Bergman Blix 2022; Missalle 2023). The empirical research led, conducted, or inspired by Blix examined various facets of courtroom dynamics, such as "formation of objectivity" by legal professionals, coordination among trial participants, and the regulation of emotions during judicial decision-making. A key aspect of the Swedish studies is this broad focus: investigating not only judges but also other courtroom actors. A wide array of research methodologies was used, including interviews, observations, case file analyses, and shadowing. Importantly, these scholars recognized that empathic responses occur at different stages of the decision-making process. In interviews with judges, the researchers posed questions and received responses directly or indirectly related to the role of empathy in judicial work. Additionally, observations of hearings focused on empathy-related behavior by justices as well as other parties, offering valuable insights into how empathy is manifested in real-time courtroom interactions.

While these studies have provided significant advantages—such as comprehensive data collection and a detailed exploration of empathy in the judicial context—they (unsurprisingly) could not provide an exhaustive examination. Additionally, the definition of empathy employed—shaping both the design of the studies and the interpretation of data—is centered on emotions and encompasses what is referred to as "easy empathy" (see Chapter 3). Specifically, Bergman Blix (2019: 164) defined the term as "a process of emotionally tuning into others' emotions while imaginatively taking the perspective of the other." It would be useful to understand the rationale behind this specific interpretation of empathy and whether the judges and other participants in the study shared this understanding or held different ones.

In addition to the Swedish studies, Sharyn Roach Anleu and Kathy Mack (2017: 63–70, 2021b: 70–83) have also offered insight into the perspective of justices regarding empathy. That research was based on an extensive dataset concerning the Australian judiciary collected over more than two decades. Roach Anleu and Mack presented not only the results of quantitative gauging of how judges prioritize empathy in their work (compared to other merits) but also qualitative information drawn from in-depth interviews with judges, again highlighting empathy in the juridical domain. However, it is important to note that—in this research, too—the denotation of empathy in the questionnaire is vague, leaving room for interpretation in the minds of respondents. Highly plausible is that the word "empathy" encompasses a spectrum of meanings for judges; crucially, one possible connotation, "sympathy," was another quality assessed in the questionnaire. Furthermore, while asking judges to prioritize empathy provides an interesting perspective on their preferences, that step could not reach the more subtle or disputed issues pertaining to empathy's place in the courthouse. Additionally, as in the Swedish case, the interviews covered various components of the judges' work and were not exclusively focused on the topic of empathy. Our observations here are not meant as a critique of Anleu and Mack's studies, but rather as recognition of the fact that their study aimed at mapping diverse aspects of judges' roles and perspectives, not solely empathy.

The latest research delving into the viewpoints of justices was conducted by Ciarán Barry and his colleagues (2023) who explored the nuanced emotion management strategies (see also Wojciechowski et al. 2015; Snider Katie et al. 2022) employed by Irish judges in their interactions with jurors. Using qualitative research methods, this team conducted 22 interviews with judges, uncovering how these legal professionals have navigated the complexities of emotional labor in the courtroom. The study reveals that judges develop and refine relevant practices and reactions through informal, indirect cues, both verbal and nonverbal, often learned and habituated over time. A key finding was the delicate balance these judges maintained between performing neutrality and subtly expressing empathy in their interactions with jurors. While emphasizing the importance of impartiality and objectivity, the judges interviewed highlighted their strategic use of empathy, particularly at the beginning of a trial. They reported that taking the standpoint of prospective jurors is crucial in smoothing the proceedings, reducing juror stress, and fostering a positive connection with members of the jury. Empathy, in this context, is portrayed as a cognitive process, carefully integrated into the larger framework of emotion management. In this case, judges have used empathy to build trust and establish a bond with jurors, often in a subtle, "by-the-way" manner. This approach helped create a courtroom environment in which jurors felt recognized and supported, which, in turn, could enhance their performance and overall experience during a trial. Moreover, the study emphasized that judges are mindful of juror well-being: The former apply empathy to demonstrate concern for the emotional state of the latter. Such empathetic engagement is not merely about understanding a juror's outlook but is also an essential tool for managing the emotional dynamics in a courtroom. Barry et al. have thus illustrated empathy as an interactionally embedded practice, integral to the broader emotional labor that judges perform in their judicial roles.

The Swedish, Australian, and Irish cases do provide certain valuable information on the perspective of judges toward empathy. Significantly, however, judges themselves—mostly Americans who are also legal scholars—do occasionally share their thoughts and experiences on this topic. Among them, Denny Chin (2012), a judge who served in the United States Court of Appeals for the Second Circuit, provided his views with respect to empathy. Defining it as "the capacity to understand and appreciate the perspective of others," Chin considered empathy "an essential characteristic for a judge" (2012: 1564). Drawing on his experiences on the bench, he specifically addressed the role of empathy (and emotions) in sentencing. For him, empathy makes the entire process more humane, and thus Chin aimed to obtain a more comprehensive picture when deciding on someone's life. Undoubtedly, such testimonies are critical and enrich our understanding of empathy in the context of judging. They are, however, not an outcome of standardized and planned exploration, and certainly do not compensate for a dearth of far-reaching investigations into the stances toward empathy taken by justices in their courtrooms.

Conclusions

Vital at this point is emphasis on three key points regarding the current state of research into the relationship between empathy and judicial decision-making. First, there is a strikingly limited number of studies that provides direct access to judges' perceptions of empathy's role—its advantages or disadvantages in their work. Given that empathy, in a broader sense, often signifies "perspective-taking," it is noteworthy that much of the literature fails to take into account whether judges use or disuse empathy and why. This omission leads to an "anti-empathetic" discourse in legal studies that marginalizes the voices and experiences of those who play so pivotal a role in the delivery of justice. A consequence is an urgent need for research that seeks to understand what judges themselves think and experience concerning empathy, including their own definitions of the concept and how they perceive its role in their work. Without incorporating their points of view, any attempts to develop a comprehensive understanding of empathy in the judicial realm—or to implement reforms aimed at modifying empathy's influence in the judicial process—remain incomplete and inadequate.

Second, it is worth highlighting that the majority of studies in this field focus primarily on empathy's functioning in common law systems. While examples from Sweden and, to some extent, Ireland, offer notable exceptions, that research stands out precisely due to an otherwise common law–dominated discourse. The relatively narrow focus of studies completed heretofore only underscores the importance of expanding the study of judicial empathy to civil law systems and other jurisdictions where different legal structures and cultural contexts may distinctly shape how empathy is understood and applied in judicial settings.

Third, the study of empathy in law—particularly in juridical settings—is not limited to legal scholarship but also spans across psychology, social psychology, sociology, and philosophy. That interdisciplinarity complicates discerning how empathy's place and role in judicial decision-making are comprehended by justices. After all, different fields will define empathy differently and emphasize different aspects. For instance, some studies prioritize the cognitive dimensions of empathy, while others focus on the emotional ones—or attempt to balance both. This diversity of perspectives underscores the need for caution in imposing any single conceptualization of empathy onto a judge's way of arriving at a verdict. Instead, it is vital to remain open to judges' own understandings, viewpoints, and conceptualizations of empathy, allowing their voices to inform the academic discourse.

This volume was inspired by a call to address these three issues as well as the general state of affairs in understanding the connections between empathy and law, and specifically between empathy and the making of a judicial decision. In consequence, the ensuing sections of the book at hand present an empirical study that captures the way empathy is understood by judges in contemporary Poland, their views about the place of empathy in legal decision-making, and their experiences with empathy in the courtroom.

References

Bandes, Susan A. 1996. "Empathy, Narrative, and Victim Impact Statements." *University of Chicago Law Review* 63: 361–412.

Bandes, Susan A. 2009. "Empathetic Judging and the Rule of Law." *Cardozo Law Review De Novo* 133–148.

Bandes, Susan A. 2011. "Moral Imagination in Judging." *Washburn Law Review* 51: 1–24.

Bandes, Susan A. and Neal Feigenson. 2021. "Empathy and Remote Legal Proceedings." *Southwestern Law Review* 51: 20.

Bandes, Susan A. et al (eds.). 2021. *Research Handbook on Law and Emotion.* Northampton, MA: Edward Elgar Publishing.

Barry, Colette et al. 2023. "The Emotional Labour of Judges in Jury Trials." *Journal of Law and Society* 50: 477–499.

Bergman Blix, Stina. 2019. "Different Roads to Empathy: Stage Actors and Judges as Polar Cases." *Emotions and Society* 1(2): 163–180.

Bergman Blix, Stina and Åsa Wettergren. 2018. *Professional Emotions in Court.* London: Routledge.

Bladini, Moa and Stina Bergman Blix. 2022. "The Judge Under Pressure: Fostering Objectivity by Abandoning the Myth of Dispassion." In *Judicial Independence Under Threat*, edited by Dimitrios Giannoulopoulos and Yvonne McDermott. 223–240. London: Oxford University Press.

Booth, Tracey. 2019. "Family Violence and Judicial Empathy: Managing Personal Cross Examination in Australian Family Law Proceedings." *Oñati Socio-Legal Series* 9(5): 702–725.

Brennan, Reason. 1988. "Passion, and 'The Progress of the Law'." *Cardozo Law Review* 10(1): 3–25.
Chin, Denny. 2012. "Sentencing: A Role for Empathy." *University of Pennsylvania Law Review* 160: 1561–1584.
Colby, Thomas B. 2012. "In Defense of Judicial Empathy." *Minnesota Law Review* 96: 1945–2015.
Colker, Ruth. 1989. "Feminism, Theology, and Abortion: Toward Love, Compassion, and Wisdom." *California Law Review* 77: 1011–1075.
Cormack, Warren. 2021. "Reassessing the Judicial Empathy Debate: How Empathy Can Distort and Improve Criminal Sentencing." *Mitchell Hamline Law Review* 47(4): 81–110.
Cornell, Jennifer L. 2022. "Reading Cases for Empathy." *University of St. Thomas Law Journal* 17(4): 772–784.
Corso, Lucia. 2014. "Empathy in the Interpretation of Constitutional Rights." *Ratio Juris* 27: 94–115. https://doi.org/10.1111/raju.12037
Eliasson, Michelle N. and Dana DeHart. 2023. "Police Officers' Empathy Toward Victims: A Question of Innocence." *International Journal of Police Science* 2(1). https://doi.org/10.56331/487529/IJPS3
Fissell, Brenner. 2016. "Modern Critiques of Judicial Empathy: A Revised Intellectual History." *Michigan State Law Review* 817: 817–851.
Gaakeer, Jeanne. 2019. "Empathy Revisited: Who's in Narrative Control?" In *Judging from Experience: Law, Praxis, Humanities*, Edinburgh: Edinburgh University Press. 205–228. https://doi.org/10.1515/9781474442503-013
Gallacher, Ian. 2012. "Thinking Like Non-Lawyers: Why Empathy Is a Core Lawyering Skill and Why Legal Education Should Change to Reflect Its Importance." *College of Law Faculty Scholarship* 6: 1–49.
Gascón-Cuenca, Andrés. 2018. "Acknowledging the Relevance of Empathy in Clinical Legal Education: Some Proposals from the Experience of the University of Brescia (IT) and Valencia (ESP)." *International Journal of Clinical Legal Education* 25.
Glynn, Adam. N. and Maya Sen. 2015. "Identifying Judicial Empathy: Does Having Daughters Cause Judges to Rule for Women's Issues?" *American Journal of Political Science* 59(1): 37–54.
Haney, Craig. 2004. "Condemning the Other in Death Penalty Trials: Biographical Racism, Structural Mitigation and the Empathic Divide." *DePaul Law Review* 53: 1557–1589.
Henderson, Lynne. 1987. "Legality and Empathy." *Michigan Law Review* 85(6): 1574–1653.
Henderson, Lynne. 1988. "The Dialogue of Heart and Head." *Cardozo Law Review* 10: 123–148.
Hoffman, Martin L. (2011). "Empathy, Justice, and the Law." In *Empathy: Philosophical and Psychological Perspectives*, edited by Amy Coplan and Peter Goldie. 230–254. Oxford: Oxford University Press.
Hunter, Rosemary. 2013. "Contesting the Dominant Paradigm: Feminist Critiques of Liberal Legalism." In *The Ashgate Research Companion to Feminist Legal Theory*, edited by Margaret Davies and Vanessa Munro. 13–30. Farnham: Ashgate.
Johnson, James D. et al. 2002. "Rodney King and O. J. Revisited: The Impact of Race and Defendant Empathy Induction on Judicial Decisions." *Journal of Applied Social Psychology* 32: 1208–1223. https://doi.org/10.1111/j.1559-1816.2002.tb01432.x
Jones, Emma. 2017. "Empathy: An Essential Element of Legal Practice or 'Never the Twain Shall Meet'?" *International Journal of the Legal Profession* 25(1).
Karni, Perlman. 2018. "Settlement Adjudication and Judicial Responsiveness: The Choice Between a Wide and a Narrow Model." In *The Responsive Judge*, edited

by Tania Sourdin and Archie Zariski. 61–86. Cham: Springer. https://doi.org/10.1007/978-981-13-1023-2_361-86

Lawton, Amy et al. 2022. "Do We Want a Human First, and a Lawyer Second? Developing Law Student Empathy Through Clinical Legal Education." *International Journal of Clinical Legal Education* 29: 4–31.

Lee, Rebecca K. 2014. "Judging Judges: Empathy as the Litmus Test for Impartiality." *University of Cincinnati Law Review* 82: 145–206.

Lewicka-Zelent, Agnieszka and Agnieszka Pytka. 2020. "Prison Service Employee's Empathy and Professional Burnout." *PS* 35(6): 99–116. https://doi.org/10.5604/01.3001.0014.5740

Lynch, Mona and Craig Haney. 2011. "Mapping the Racial Bias of the White Male Capital Juror: Jury Composition and the 'Empathic Divide'." *Law & Society Review* 45: 69–102.

Maroney, Terry A. 2011. "The Persistent Cultural Script of Judicial Dispassion." *California Law Review* 99: 629–681.

Maroney, Terry A. and Phillip Ackerman-Lieberman. 2014. "As a Father Shows Compassion for His Children." *Journal of Law, Religion and State* 2(3): 240–275.

McArdle, Andrea L. 2012. "Using a Narrative Lens to Understand Empathy and How It Matters in Judging." *Legal Communication & Rhetoric: JALWD* 9: 173–206.

Missalle, Alessandra. 2023. *Emotions in Legal Decisions: The Construction of Objective Narratives in Italian Criminal Trials.* Uppsala: Uppsala University Press.

Morawetz, Thomas. 1996. "Empathy and Judgment." *Yale Journal of Law and Humanities* 8: 517–526.

Moyer, Laura and Susan B. Haire. 2015. "Trailblazers and those that Followed: Personal Experiences, Gender, and Judicial Empathy." *Law & Society Review* 49(3): 665–689.

Nussbaum, Martha. 1996. "Compassion: The Basic Social Emotion." *Social Philosophy and Policy* 13(1): 27–58. https://doi.org/10.1017/S0265052500001515

Nussbaum, Martha. 2013. *Political Emotions: Why Love Matters for Justice.* Cambridge, MA: The Belknap Press of Harvard University Press.

Pearson, Megan. 2020. "Empathy and Procedural Justice in Clash of Rights Cases." *Oxford Journal of Law and Religion* 9(2): 350–371.

Pemberton, Antony. 2016. "Empathy for Victims in Criminal Justice: Revisiting Susan Bandes in Victimology." In *Emotional Dynamics of Law and Legal Discourse*, edited by Heather Conway and John Stannard. 105–127. London: Hart Publishers.

Posick, Chad et al. 2014. "More Than a Feeling: Integrating Empathy Into the Study of Lawmaking, Lawbreaking, and Reactions to Lawbreaking." *International Journal of Offender Therapy and Comparative Criminology* 58(1): 5–26. https://doi.org/10.1177/0306624X12465411

Posner, Richard A. 2008. *How Judges Think.* Cambridge, MA: Harvard University Press.

Reichman, Amnon. 2006. "Law, Literature, and Empathy: Between Withholding and. Reserving Judgment." *Journal of Legal Education* 56(2): 296–319.

Roach Anleu, Sharyn and Kathy Mack. 2017. *Performing Judicial Authority in the Lower Courts.* London: Palgrave Macmillan.

Roach Anleu, Sharyn and Kathy Mack. 2021a. *Judging and Emotion a Socio-Legal Analysis.* London: Routledge.

Roach Anleu, Sharyn and Kathy Mack. 2021b. "Emotion Work as Judicial Work." In *The Judge, the Judiciary and the Court: Individual, Collegial and Institutional Judicial Dynamics in Australia*, edited by Gabriele Appleby and Andrew Lynch. 143–162. Cambridge: Cambridge University Press.

Rosenberg, Joshua D. 2002. "Teaching Empathy in Law School." *University of San Francisco Law Review* 36(3): 621–657.

Rużyczka, Katarzyna. 2023. "Should Judges Be Empathic? The Place of Judges' Empathy in Therapeutic Jurisprudence." *Archiwum Filozofii Prawa i Filozofii Społecznej* 35(2): 53–64.

Slote, Michael. 2013. "Empathy, Law and Justice." In *Law, Virtue and Justice*, edited by Amalia Amaya and Ho Hock Lai. 279–292. Oxford: Hart Publishing.

Snider Katie, M. et al. 2022. "Judges' Emotion: An Application of the Emotion Regulation Process Model." *Psychiatry, Psychology and Law* 29(2): 256–273.

Spivak, Benjamin et al. 2018. "Measuring Empathy in Undergraduate Law Students: Examining the Factorial Validity of the Jefferson Scale of Empathy—Law Students (JSE-LS)." *International Journal of Law and Psychiatry* 58: 143–149.

Stępień, Mateusz. 2021. "On the Relationship between Judicial Empathy and the Integrity of Judges." *Krytyka Prawa. Niezależne Studia Nad Prawem* 13(3): 98–113.

Weinberg, Jill D. and Laura Beth Nielsen. 2012. "Examining Empathy: Discrimination, Experience, and Judicial Decision-making." *Southern California Law Review* 85: 313–352.

Wettergren, Åsa and Stina Bergman Blix. 2016. "Empathy and Objectivity in the Legal Process: The Case of Swedish Prosecutors." *Journal of Scandinavian Studies in Criminology and Crime Prevention* 17: 19–35.

Wilczek-Rużyczka, Ewa and Michał Kupczyk. 2021. "Level of Empathy and Severity of Psychopathic Traits in Medical, Law and Psychology Students." *Acta Neuropsychologica* 19(4): 411–426.

Winick, Bruce J. 2002–2003. "Therapeutic Jurisprudence and Problem-Solving Courts." *Fordham Urban Law Journal* 30: 1055: 1103.

Wojciechowski, Maciej et al. 2015. "Emotional Labour of Judges." *Archiwum Filozofii Prawa i Filozofii Społecznej* 1(10): 97–110.

Wood, Jane et al. 2014. "'I Know How They Must Feel': Empathy and Judging Defendants." *The European Journal of Psychology Applied to Legal Context* 6(1): 37–43.

Zipursky, Benjamin. 2012. "Anti-Empathy and Dispassionateness in Adjudication." In *Passions and Emotions: NOMOS LIII*, edited by James E. Fleming. 304–314. New York: NYU Press.

2 Methodology, study context, and challenges

Mateusz Stępień

Introduction

Tightly focused on empathy and law, this chapter explores the methodological choices and primary challenges that arose over the course of our empirical research into the empathic perspectives and experiences of judges in Poland. Explained is the reasoning behind the methods selected; outlined are the problems and limitations of the research techniques employed. Crucial for understanding our research and its objectives, however, is the broader context—that is, the structure and qualities of the Polish judicial system and the essential, professional prerequisites for becoming a judge. Understanding the idiosyncrasies of the Polish system is vital for effective incorporation of the collected data into the expanding body of research into empathy in legal decision-making. Moreover, the reader should be familiarized with certain touchstones of the broader sociopolitical context. That context included harassment of certain justices, undertaken by the government ruling between 2015 and 2023—a fact that likely influenced responses.

Courts in Poland: their role and significance

The Polish legal system follows the civil law tradition, and, consequently, the judiciary displays typical characteristics of such a jurisdiction (see Merryman, Pérez-Perdomo 2018). The government in the Republic of Poland (per Article 10 of its Constitution dated 2 April 1997) is built on the separation and balance of powers between the legislative, executive, and judicial branches. The judicial authorities encompass the courts and tribunals, at the top of which hierarchy is the Constitutional Tribunal, responsible for scrutinizing the constitutionality of laws. Within the judicial system, there are military, administrative, and so-called ordinary courts, as well as the Supreme Court. The last of these oversees the ordinary courts, manages annulments or reversals of specific decisions delivered in courts of appeal, and, since 2018, handles extraordinary complaints, which can be applied to valid, final verdicts. Yet with their wide-ranging authority, it is in the ordinary courts (hereinafter referred

DOI: 10.4324/9781003546580-3

to simply as "courts") that citizens usually deal with issues like divorces, adoptions, contract breaches, offenses, and crimes.

Among the three principal types of ordinary courts in Poland, the regional courts (*sądy rejonowe*, encompassing several communes) hold extensive original jurisdiction power, serve as the initial encounter with the system, and handle most cases with the exception of those specifically assigned elsewhere. These courts are organized into specialized divisions based on the types of cases they handle, including civil, criminal, land registry, commercial bankruptcy, family and juvenile, or labor law. Certain litigation is handled by more specialized institutions such as Intellectual Property Courts and the Competition and Consumer Protection Court. Regional courts, serving as the main trial courts, often handle a variety of cases involving many individuals, especially witnesses. Establishing the facts in the cases leads to a high level of human interaction within the courtroom, frequently accompanied by emotional demonstrations by the individuals present. Regional courts process a large number of cases daily, and the scope of distinguishing ritual and symbolism is often limited due to the smaller and older courtrooms, but the number of contentious legal disputes and wranglings is reduced in comparison to higher judicial tiers. Typically, with the exclusion of specific labor and family cases (where lay judges are selected for a defined period, rather than on an ad hoc basis), a single judge manages cases, engaging directly with the participants. The COVID-19 pandemic resulted in a notable decrease in the involvement of lay judges and a preference for closed over open sessions; currently, the situation is gradually returning to the prepandemic status quo. Next are the district courts (*sądy okręgowe*), which serve both the first and second levels: They handle major civil and criminal cases in their original jurisdiction, but also supervise the appeals process for judgments from regional courts. The reach of their jurisdiction covers several smaller ones. The third category includes appellate courts (*sądy apelacyjne*), which lack primary jurisdiction and can only hear appeals from an area with at least two district courts. In most cases, they do not investigate the evidence, rely on the information gathered by the lower courts, and chiefly operate on the basis of written materials.

To gain a comprehensive understanding of the Polish system's scope at the previously described tiers, it is important to note that, in 2021, during the core research period, there was a total of 375 such courts in the Polish system. These included 318 regional, 46 district, and 11 appellate courts (GUS 2022). Functioning therein were 6,015 judges in regional courts, 2,682 in district courts, and 459 in appellate courts. Additionally, there were 410 individuals serving as judicial assessors, who handle only specific types of legal matters. After practicing for about 2–3 years, they are eligible to compete to fill judicial vacancies; the most typical career path to a judgeship in Poland is by first serving as an assessor.

Court proceedings in Poland are regulated by procedural codes, with the most crucial ones being the Criminal Procedure Act of 1997 and the Civil Procedure Act of 1965 (both extensively amended; see Bednarek 2014;

Ryan 2016). Referring to the latter, there are two types of civil procedures in Poland: contentious and noncontentious proceedings. Generally speaking, the first is adversarial, while the second (theoretically not involving antagonistic, conflicted parties) is less adversarial. As for the former procedure, the criminal combines inquisitorial and adversarial elements, following a two-party model (an accused individual versus a public prosecutor), complemented by a highly involved judge. In cases of severe crimes, professional judges are accompanied on the bench by two or three lay judges who are selected for a period of four years. In particular, the trial judge in Poland plays a dynamic part in civil and criminal cases, setting these judges apart from those in common law systems. Even with several reforms aimed at including more adversarial elements into both civil and criminal procedures, Polish trials are still characterized by significant involvement of the judge(s). These justices often take the lead in the proceedings—including the evidentiary phase during which they actively question witnesses.

Returning to the process of becoming a judge, it is crucial to understand that selection and career advancement in the Polish judiciary resemble a civil service model (see Mistygacz 2020). Previously, specialized training for those who passed the entrance exam was conducted in appellate courts. Individuals currently aspiring to become judges undergo extensive, specialized training, typically lasting a minimum of ten years, including the completion of a five-year (omitting the bachelor level) master's degree in law. With this as the preliminary step toward a career in the legal professions, aspiring judges must successfully pass a highly competitive entrance exam to gain admission into the state-managed National School of Judiciary and Public Prosecution—providing a three-year, centralized, and standardized education—that was established in 2009. After rigorous training and a final examination, successful candidates are allowed to apply for open positions in the judiciary. As mentioned earlier, they serve as judicial assessors before being appointed to career positions. There is also the possibility of being appointed to a judgeship after practicing other legal professions for some period. In both cases, candidates for open positions in the judiciary are assessed and recommended by the National Council of the Judiciary. After receiving a positive evaluation, they are nominated by the president of the Republic of Poland for an unspecified tenure.

Significantly, the positivist tradition holds considerable influence in Poland with respect to how judges are trained, perceive their role, and manage hearings (see Mańko 2013). Positivism is deeply rooted historically: For instance, legal professionals employed a "formalistic shield" between 1945 and 1989 to safeguard their professionalism under communism. The substantial impact of German legal traditions before (and to some extent also after) World War II has further contributed to this influence. The convergence of all these factors still shapes the role of judges and their judicial conduct. It underscores the long-standing dominance of an ideally stone-faced demeanor that manifests dispassion, employs highly formal communication, and maintains a high power distance (Dudek, Stępień 2021).

The political and social context

The research project was conducted under extraordinary circumstances. This refers not only to the challenges posed by the COVID-19 pandemic, which impacted the judiciary as well as the organization of the research itself, but also to the sociopolitical context the research team faced while exploring the perspectives and views of judges in Poland. For several years, individual justices and the courts have been at the center of political and social disputes in Poland—not just as adjudicators dealing with disagreements, conflicts, and turmoil but also as the primary subjects of such disputes. While the limits of this book preclude a detailed presentation of this unprecedented attack on the judiciary, it is essential to unveil some of the context and seriously consider whether, and how, that situation has influenced the research and potentially its findings (see Sadurski 2019; Zoll, Wortham 2019).

The story begins in the autumn of 2015. Shortly after coming to power, a parliamentary majority led by the right-wing Law and Justice party (*Prawo i Sprawiedliwość*, PiS) initiated deep and controversial reforms to the legal system, primarily targeting the judiciary. The first major battlefield was the Constitutional Tribunal, endowed with significant powers, including the authority to review the constitutionality of legal acts. After gaining control of that tribunal, the ruling party turned its attention to the first-tier courts, consisting of approximately 10,000 judges. Those justices who did not accept the constitutionally questionable transformations and a commandeering of the tribunal were often characterized in government narratives as an "unaccountable," untouchable occupational "caste" (for comparative insight regarding Central Europe, see Čuroš 2023). In the summer of 2017, the government introduced legislative bills pertaining to the appointment of judges, the organization of lower courts, and a comprehensive reorganization of the Supreme Court. Concurrently, the government directly and indirectly conducted an aggressive propaganda campaign against judges, emphasizing issues such as judicial error and alleged misconduct (see Stępień, Radomska 2024). Although two out of the three bills were—following unprecedented public protest and the mobilization of judges (see Matthes 2022; Puleo, Coman 2024)—vetoed by the president, ultimately all three projected reforms upsetting judiciary autonomy came into effect by the beginning of January 2018. In general, the measures introduced through these legislative changes were perceived as attempts to exert even greater political control over the judiciary and undermine its independence (see Szwed 2023).

These shakeups exacerbated a crisis within the judicial branch and introduced new areas of conflict. For instance, one bill aimed to reshape the National Council of the Judiciary, which nominates judges. The reigning majority reinterpreted the constitutional provision regarding the appointment of council members, granting significantly more power to the legislature (the *Sejm*, the lower house of parliament). Previously, representatives of all justices in Poland were selected by self-governing judicial bodies. After this change, representatives to the National Council were selected by the ruling majority, expanding its control over judicial appointments and promotions. Most legal experts considered this move unconstitutional.

Furthermore, subsequent decisions regarding judicial appointments made by this ostensibly unconstitutional National Council of the Judiciary began to be contested, and the status of newly appointed judges (known as *neosędziowie*, "neo-judges") was widely questioned due to errors in the nomination process. In reaction to queries about the legal standing of the "neo-judges," the parliamentary majority stymied the doubt-casting via disciplinary measures against the judges who raised relevant issues with the European Court of Justice. Consequently, issues with the PiS-blessed appointees (as well as other problems) reached the European Court of Human Rights; the crisis escalated as the right-wing government began to question certain competencies of EU institutions as well as the primacy of EU law for a member state. Here it should be added that the new center-left government installed in December 2023 has not resolved these issues, largely because the president, who possesses veto power over legislative bills, remains aligned with the Law and Justice party. Moreover, the task of restoring the rule of law has become a source of new controversies, as it is challenging to achieve that restoration while strictly adhering to the letter of the law—especially in such a complex legal and political environment.

At this point it should be disclosed that it was precisely amidst this extremely heated and partisan atmosphere that our research on empathy in the decision-making of justices was conducted. We can speculate about the impact of that general backdrop with its specific political pressures on the actual role of empathy within the judiciary. On one hand, the growing turmoil within the judiciary—coupled with factors such as an overwhelming caseload and struggles to safeguard the most important judicial values—would likely limit the available space and incentives for empathy and diminish interest in soft skills overall. In this sense, the crisis would affect the actual extent of empathy usage by judges in their work and, in turn, could translate into how judges perceive and think about such matters. Faced by more urgent, pressing challenges, judges' interest in the research and willingness to participate would be low. On the other hand, as judges realized that the judiciary needed to be more responsive to citizens and society, and as they came to care about how the public perceives them, there would be a growing need for more empathic judging—in contrast to the traditional stone-faced model. In this vein, one could expect that the crisis would expand the use of empathy by judges as part of a people-oriented approach to dispensing justice: framing empathy as an essential element of justice and judicial decision-making.

All that together could influence how judges framed this subject in their responses to our queries. Considering the two just-described tendencies, the actual impact of the sociopolitical background on the research cannot be measured by participant interest and willingness to contribute to our study along with the way participants framed their narratives on judicial empathy.

One could speculate that this specific context triggered judges to present, in good faith, a more positive view of themselves, as they were under attack. The question of whether and how all these factors shaped the sampling will be discussed. It should also be mentioned that during the interviews, judges primarily focused on their actual experiences and views related to empathy and judging, often backing away from the complex sociopolitical milieux. That said, they did sometimes acknowledge the thick atmosphere without providing details or expressing complaints.

Methodology applied

It is crucial to recognize that despite the wealth of empirical studies on empathy, many rely on existing psychometric indices to measure it. These instruments typically ask individuals to rate themselves (or others) on various behaviors, feelings, motives, or attitudes, leading to a range of scores that are aggregated by researchers as a measure of empathy. However, these scales often fall short in capturing the specificity of empathic reactions in specific social settings (e.g., occupational milieux) and fail to provide insight into respondents' own conceptualizations of empathy. What is mostly missing is the emic perspective. Given the research interest in understanding the views and experiences of judges regarding empathy in their professional role, a research technique offering a view into their world was necessary. Qualitative research, particularly in-depth interviews (IDIs) (see, e.g., Lee 2017), was deemed most suitable for grasping judges' perceptions, opinions, sentiments, and experiences. This method allowed for a nuanced exploration of how these persons conceptualize and practice empathy in their work—even if this was not always apparent to them. IDIs were chosen as the primary data collection method, as they are well-suited for uncovering authentic sensitivities and practices related to subtle subjects like empathy. Judges were invited to participate in structured interviews with a set of predetermined questions designed to explore various dimensions of empathy and its relationship to the act of judging. This choice was justified by the need to understand complex and often intangible aspects of the professional lives of justices.

In selecting interviewees, the starting point was to embrace the diverse viewpoints expressed by judges working in different types of courts. Initially, the snowball method was utilized to recruit participants (Handcock, Gile 2011), leveraging existing contacts within the judiciary to identify potential interviewees. After interviewing, these individuals were asked to help in contacting others. This strategy was only partially successful and bore its own disadvantages, such as limited access to certain subgroups and circles. As the study progressed, an additional method was employed: random selection of courts from a pre-established pool, followed by the sending of open invitations to judges from these selected courts to participate in the project. At this stage, the research team did not control the dissemination of the invitations within the specific courts. In fact, the heads of the courts responded variously to the call. Some completely ignored the invitation, while others fairly distributed it and even joined the research themselves. Although the two-step method of selecting participants was better than relying on one, the resultant sample was not as diverse and representative as initially hoped. However, it did turn out to be more uniform and better representative of a particular segment of the judiciary.

Due to the impact of the COVID-19 pandemic, the decision was made to pivot to online IDIs (see Salmons 2014; Howlett 2022). In most cases, our interlocutors were in their homes, with interviews held after work hours. This was an important factor that, we believe, enabled us to establish connections and sometimes bonds with the participants, as we chatted in environments safe for them. Notably, in many interviews, family members and even pets intervened in the conversation, which, frankly, was positive, as it created an atmosphere contrary to formality and seriousness. Additionally, the venues where the interviews were conducted lacked the symbolic elements of professional and judicial culture. This kind of setting worked well to enhance sincerity in expressing opinions and sharing experiences connected with empathy. Strangely, due to forces beyond our control, the face-to-face interviews we had initially planned were replaced by online interviews, which, in fact, facilitated more honest conversations. It is likely that the virtual yet familiar comfort zones in which interviewees were situated shaped the depth of the data collected.

Interviewees were free to speak, in their own words, about the phenomenon in question. The interviewer showed interest in responses and encouraged elaboration by sharing personal experiences. Open-ended questions with prompts were used to guide the conversation toward specific topics; the interviewer was flexible in the phrasing of questions, asking follow-up questions, or requesting examples. The IDI technique allows for great pliancy.

Moreover, the length of the interviews varied depending on factors such as participant time constraints and the depth of the narratives provided. The average duration was approximately 100 minutes, with some extending up to two and a half hours. All interviewees consented to recording, which enhanced the accuracy of result reporting. The data collected from the interviews were transcribed and then coded for content analysis.

An initial reading of the transcripts disclosed significant differences in the views and experiences of judges from the family court division. Their work is deeply entwined with the emotions of others, fundamental human values, and profound conflicts involving children. The approach to empathy of these judges was markedly different from that of other judges. This observation prompted the research team to investigate further and to initiate a new empirical research stage not foreseen earlier. We reached out to the Family Judges Association, which assisted us in organizing both online and in-person focus group interviews (FGIs) in 2023. Fifteen judges, exclusively from family courts, participated in three focus groups. Moderators posed questions related to the unique context of family courts, aiming to investigate more deeply the experiences and perspectives of these judges in order to enrich the IDI dataset. The book at hand bases its findings on the basis of the IDIs.

Sample demographics and type of analysis

Interviews took place between mid-2021 and early 2022, with over 40 conducted in total. However, only 37 of these were included in the data analysis due to technical issues with recordings and internet connections. Prior to the central interviewing phase, a pilot study was conducted with three judges in order to critically assess the questions and their sequence in the interview guide. Feedback from those three judges was instrumental in refining the questions, making them clearer and more tailored to the participants.

The interviewed judges represented diverse specializations: civil (14), family (9), criminal (8), commercial (5), and labor (1). All but three worked in regional courts, which is significant because trial court proceedings, with increased interactions and the significance of the human element, offer more opportunities for judges to exhibit empathic reactions. The sample also included four presidents of court divisions, who oversaw both judicial and administrative functions; this provided a broader viewpoint on the use of empathy in the judiciary. In terms of gender, the sample comprised 17 women and 20 men. The participants had an average of nearly 16 years of experience as judges, ranging from 30 years to 0.4 years behind the bench. This experience level means that the opinions and insights shared largely came from judges who had witnessed significant changes and reforms in the judiciary over time. Many of them had also worked in different court divisions or held various positions throughout their careers. For citation purposes and the protection of anonymity, a number (1–37) in square brackets will indicate the specific justice being quoted in the text (see Table 2.1).

As we obtained only a relatively small sample, questions arise about what motivated these judges to participate in the research and how emblematic their views and opinions are. Referring to the first issue, one can easily pinpoint factors that possibly directed judges away from responding to our call for interviewees: a huge case overload; sociopolitical pressures directing their attention to things other than research participation; the utter novelty of the subject, which could have been seen as neither the most important nor complex; the effect of judicial dispassion, which dismisses such topics out of hand; and the lack of a research participation habit to reflect upon the judiciary. This makes the opposite question all the more interesting: What motivated some judges to invest their precious time and energy in an affirmative response to a call for participation?

Broadly simplifying, we can roughly categorize judges who participated into four groups: a) those inclined to depart from the stone-faced model (and its implications) and to do so actively in practice; looking at the bigger picture, the participating individuals could also be seen as those not against what a symbolic call for change has entailed, including the means to express critique

Table 2.1 Demographic characteristics

No.	*Sex*	*Court division*	*Work experience as a judge (in years)*
1	M	Criminal	30
2	M	Commercial	8
3	F	Family	13
4	F	Criminal	20
5	M	Commercial	9
6	M	Civil, commercial, family (appellate)	28
7	M	Civil	7
8	M	Criminal	19
9	M	Commercial	19
10	M	Civil	0.4
11	F	Commercial	27
12	M	Criminal	20
13	M	Civil	18
14	F	Criminal	16
15	F	Family	11
16	F	Civil	20
17	F	Civil	15
18	M	Civil	16
19	M	Civil, family (appellate)	13
20	M	Family	20
21	M	Family	20
22	M	Family	20
23	F	Family	23
24	M	Criminal	18
25	M	Civil	10
26	F	Labor	18
27	F	Family	6
28	F	Criminal	15
29	F	Civil	30
30	F	Commercial	21
31	F	Family	9
32	F	Civil	6
33	F	Civil	17
34	M	Criminal (appellate)	14
35	F	Family	6
36	M	Civil	0.5
37	M	Civil	25

against some judicial orthodoxies; b) those who desired to voice their opinions outright, sensing that their perspectives had remained unheard; c) court presidents or division chiefs who might feel some kind of obligation to participate in the research; and d) those curious about the whole process of research and willing to check how it works.

It became evident that our sample, while not entirely unrepresentative, did lack more critical voices concerning empathy in judicial decision-making. As will be shown, all the judges who voluntarily chose to participate in the study conveyed a positive stance toward the application of empathy by judges, yet their perceptions about empathy's role and its limits differed widely. They openly acknowledged that they occasionally, to varying degrees, employ empathy over the course of their work. In a sense—and keeping in mind that this was only a general tendency—one might say that there is a high probability that participating judges are more empathic or sensitive or care more. Taken into consideration is that the very topic might have appealed to those judges who were already interested in or felt strongly about it, potentially skewing the sample toward those more empathetically inclined. One of the interviewees [12] noticed something similar when pointing out that "I'm afraid your research might be a little bit distorted, because they rather will be carried out with people who are slightly more open [than others]."

Whereas the sample provided valuable insights, caution must be taken when generalizing the data to all judges in Poland in the early 21st century. The motivations for participation and the context in which the research was conducted do suggest that the views and opinions collected may reflect specific segments of the judiciary, rather than the entire population of judges. Future research could aim to include a more diverse spectrum of participants to enhance the representativeness and depth of understanding of judicial empathy.

Moving to the type of data analysis employed, it is important to mention that thematic analysis was chosen as the primary method for organizing and interpreting the data. This approach was selected because of its ability to "identify, analyze, and report patterns (themes) within the data" (Braun, Clarke 2006: 79). The goal was to map judges' perspectives on empathy-related subjects and to extract key themes—meanings that captured core ideas within the data in relation to the research questions, representing patterned responses or clusters within the dataset. Thematic analysis is widely used to distill extensive and varied raw data into a structured, organized format. In this study, after an initial familiarization with the transcripts, themes related to the research questions were identified, often leading to the creation of typologies based on the interviewees' views. The transcripts were then re-read, and the list of themes (and typologies) was refined and reinterpreted to provide a clearer understanding of the judges' perspectives.

Primary methodological challenges

Empirical research typically presents numerous challenges and trade-offs, and this study is no exception. It is necessary to reflect on knotty methodological issues, addressing those related to the very subject of the research, including conundrums associated with ambitious inquiries into empathy. Attention also needs to be paid to the composition of the interviewee cohort—especially considering very specialized and highly experienced judges with their potential biases and lack of reflexivity with regard to their work.

Challenges associated with studying empathy in a legal context

Interviewing judges about their perceptions of empathy and its applications in their professional lives is a tricky enterprise. Among other reasons are those associated specifically with the task judges perform and how they perform it. Before going further, it is worth citing an observation by Susan Bandes (2011: 5):

> The conversation about empathy in judging is beset with difficulties. The definitional difficulties are daunting, and bear much of the blame for the repetitive circles in which the conversation often travels. The term has multiple meanings across and even within disciplines. Some of the phenomena it describes also sometimes go by other names. And to compound the problem, the term is often interjected into legal argument without full appreciation of its ambiguities and of the difficulties of translation from fields like philosophy and psychology.

Unpacking this general diagnosis, one challenge is that the professional culture tends to regard non-emotionality as the ideal (see Maroney 2011). From this angle, judicial empathy (and especially showing empathic responses) is probably looked upon by (not only) judges with extreme caution and suspicion. Notably, empathy can be (and probably, to some extent, is) mistaken for compassion or pity or other emotions, which could be assessed as undesirable, if not wholly unwanted. Legal professionals in Poland are also largely unaccustomed to the idea of empathy in the context of law, as the relevant skillset is marginalized in their education and absent from their professional interest. For these and a multitude of other reasons, the very concept is hard to imagine, let alone discuss, in the generally legal, but especially judicial context.

Next, given the absence of a universal consensus on the nature of empathy, one problem was to probe the judges' opinions without inadvertently restricting or loosening their ideas regarding the concept about which we were asking. To put it differently, we faced the question of how to talk about empathy without imposing specific meanings and understandings. An objective was to remain open to senses that were directly or indirectly linked to empathy but still encompassed what it means in academic or nonacademic milieux. Hence a practical question was whether to use the exact word "empathy" or only ask about things typically associated with it. After all, as Bandes noted earlier, this is both a scholarly conception and an etymological term functioning in various vocabularies that may not align.

The next problem we faced was how to structure the interview, keeping in mind that—while keeping an eye on judicial empathy—it would be necessary to refer to general understandings and connotations. Exploring connections between the utilization of empathy in the private sphere as well as the professional one required a prudently prepared strategy for questioning the judges volunteering for our sample.

Balancing different pros and cons, we ultimately decided to avoid asking for a single, classic definition of empathy. Instead, we used several questions to assess an interviewee's overall understanding of empathy without yet referring to the judicial context. At this point we posed queries of the participating judges, addressing the following aspects: (a) what first thoughts come to mind about the meaning and connotations of empathy; supplementary to this, we also asked about the characteristics of an empathetic person; (b) how do they perceive the relationship between empathy and morality; (c) how do they envision the possibility of nurturing and developing empathic skills, here ascertaining whether they thought of empathy more as a trait or skill; (d) what is the relationship between empathy and compassion, considering that these two words could be misconstrued, although academic literature makes a clear distinction between the two; and (e) what experiences did they have that were related or similar to empathy, further questioning judges about how they assess their own abilities and decision-making vis-à-vis empathy. With the exception of the first one, all of the questions served to provide auxiliary information that facilitated construction and clarification of the judges' perspectives on empathy.

In the next phase of the interviews, we employed a different strategy. We asked judges to share their experiences and thoughts regarding behavior that directly related to empathy in a judicial context: (a) How do they deal with human misery, suffering, and woes typically exhibited during trials? (b) Do they respond (and how) to what happens in the courtroom? (c) Do they experience a sense of having "put themselves into someone else's shoes"? (d) Do they practice showing a human face in the courtroom?

Only after discussing these matters (and not necessarily linking this directly to empathy during the conversation), we asked our interviewees for their opinions on whether judges should or should not be empathetic. Along with other questions related to training as well as needs, we inquired about the relationship between empathy and impartiality in the judicial context. Our aim was to gather examples of concrete judicial behaviors, cases, real situations in the courtroom, and, most importantly, the intimate experiences of the judges themselves.

Naturally, the IDI methodology does bear some serious limitations, as it focuses on statements declared and verbalized by the interviewee. It should be stressed that our research project collected views as presented and could not compare them with the actual practices and observable actions taken by the justices. Indeed, judge [6], who referred to himself as a dinosaur by way of underscoring his long career, was quite aware of a disparity: "If we are going to talk about empathy, declaratively, the results will be quite good. However, in the real sphere, not necessarily." This statement is crucial, as it calls for some skepticism about the generally positive image emerging from the transcriptions. In essence, while the interviews offered valuable insights, they must be interpreted with caution, acknowledging the inherent limitations and potential biases in self-reported data.

Exploring potential, complementary avenues that could yield a more accurate picture of the empathic work of judges, several approaches could be considered. For instance, long-term shadowing or participant observation techniques could offer valuable data, although these methods are accompanied by significant logistical challenges. A more feasible method might involve the use of biographical interviews, engendering a comprehensive understanding of the experiences and changes judges undergo across their careers. Drawing inspiration from the Confucian tradition of maintaining a personal diary, persuading judges to keep diaries could be particularly stimulating. Diaries could open a unique window into the internal processes to which judges submit themselves; evinced thereby could be the subtle transformations occurring over time. This introspective approach could disclose invaluable wisdom about how empathy and other factors evolve over the intricate landscape of judges' professional lives. It is also worth considering the longitudinal study, which tracks experiences and attitudes over extended periods. That methodology could capture the gradations of judges' career developments and the impact of their professional milieu on their empathic practices. Furthermore, integrating qualitative methods with quantitative data could boost the depth as well as reliability of the findings, allowing for a more holistic image of judicial empathy.

The main challenge we encountered in research project, which forms the basis of this book, was the ambitious—perhaps overly ambitious—attempt to investigate a largely concealed phenomenon within the legal profession: the evolution of empathy throughout a judge's career. The study aimed to explore subtle, nearly imperceptible "silent transformations" (Jullien 2011) that occur over the course of a judge's professional life. While much was gleaned from the IDIs, it is essential to acknowledge their limitations in revealing the full scope of empathy labor, especially through the lens of these "silent transformations." Many of our interviewees, accustomed to functioning in an official capacity, often avoided deep, reflective contemplation of their roles. Added to this were the pressures of heavy caseloads and the risks associated with revealing the more profound layers of their decision-making processes. Although the goal was to gain a thorough understanding of judges' views on empathy, the interviews were not fully capable of uncovering the gradual, often subconscious, changes that occur over time in response to the judicial environment. Judges likely found it challenging to articulate these transformations, particularly within the confines of a single interview. As a result, while the interviews provided valuable insights, they should be considered a first step in a broader research agenda aimed at uncovering the more hidden and nuanced aspects of judicial empathy. Understanding these "silent transformations" in the empathic labor of judges would likely require a combination of methodologies. Mixed methods research could offer a richer, more detailed picture of how empathy evolves and operates within the judicial context over time.

The peculiarities of interviews with judges

For an array of reasons, judges are not typical interviewees (for a more general look into interviewing legal professionals and legal elites, see Jaremba, Mak 2014; Korkea-aho, Leino 2019; Gupta, Harvey 2022). First, judges—mostly due to the exclusive role they fulfill—are not inclined to fully disclose the details of their work, especially factors that determine their judgments. In fact, certain aspects of judicial decision-making would be especially difficult to share (see Korkea-aho, Leino 2019: 42). Additionally, it was mentioned that, when interviewing legal elites, privacy issues surface which cannot be overstepped; that, too, negatively influences the process of interviewing.

Although judges were directly informed that the research was anonymous, such assurances did not fully offset the reasons they had for not being completely transparent. Furthermore, it should be kept in mind that judges were concurrently being criticized and harassed by the ruling majority. It can be argued that—on top of other, more emblematic motivations for discretion—some self-protection mechanisms might have also come into play. Nevertheless, looking back, it seems that most of the judges interviewed did circumvent the goal of an unmistakably sharp picture of the judiciary in 21st-century Poland. Although they mentioned specific problems and provided examples of unjust judicial behavior, they were generally restrained and tactful in their critique of other judges or the profession as a whole. An overall positive atmosphere during the interviews and the uniqueness of the sample might have also been mitigating factors, but the judges were not totally silenced.

Second, judges are, in a sense, professional rationalizers—their primary task involves justifying and fortifying their views and decisions. Moreover, since much of their work consists of talking and writing, they are also accustomed to providing lengthy, elaborate treatises and discussing anything related to the judiciary freely and protractedly. Reflecting on the interviews, it was evident that, not so infrequently, justices would establish a strong, albeit ad hoc, opinion and then stick with it. Rarely did they admit that they did not know something. Fortunately, some judges did disclose their problems with understanding empathy, its nature, and the relationship between empathy and morality (e.g., "To be honest, it is very hard to answer this question [about empathy]" [10]). When it came to the judicial context, however, they seemed more certain about their opinions and stances. Potential interviewers must expect that judges will take a stand and be eager to argue for it. It is therefore advised that researchers acquire prior knowledge about how things really work in the judiciary in order to be able to pose pointed and/or inconvenient questions.

Third, judges are inclined toward coherence in their thinking and competence in their opinions, presenting these in an orderly fashion. Judges desire to be seen as sharp, intelligent, and well read. A few of our interviewees gave away that they had somewhat prepared for the interview. For instance, one judge [38] relayed that, "All in all, I prepared a little for our interview." In fact, he had made a significant effort to familiarize himself with the academic literature on empathy (e.g., distinguishing between popular and scholarly approaches, referring to the distinction between emotional and cognitive empathy). It should be noted that the instructions our respondents received ahead of their interview explicitly stated that this would be a conversational in-depth interview and thus there was no need to ready oneself. The groundwork done by some of the judges indicates that they took this seriously and wanted to provide well-informed and thought-out responses. Ultimately, however, this was both a strength and a weakness because it thwarted our yearning to record their spontaneous, unfiltered views.

Fourth and finally, judges are, in general, not prompted to continually develop a self-reflexivity about their role and their work. Due to excessive caseloads as well as various administrative matters, judges frequently miss chances to reflect upon their personal interactions within the legal domain. Consequently, with reference to the topic at hand, their understanding of their empathic work is generally insubstantial and mostly unsophisticated. The judges tended to portray their experiences in an excessively symmetrical and idealized manner. They seemed not so ready to speak of struggles, scrapes, and blemishes in their real-life experiences with balancing empathy and their professional role. A strong professional socialization further explains this bold image of their work. Interestingly (and an important takeaway from the research findings), the interview itself provided a space for some of the judges to reflect upon issues normally off their radar. One judge [23] remarked after the interview that:

> This conversation has been a bit therapeutic and head-clearing—that someone is curious about what I feel, how I feel with what I am doing. This is what I've needed very much and [this] has somehow allowed me to stop for a while during such a run—to focus for a moment on emotions—which is not happening often. Thus, this was a fruitful conversation for me.

These considerations aim at pinpointing the specificity of judges as interviewees—characteristics stemming from a unique socialization, structural determinants, and the trajectories of their careers. Ideally, this should lead to more detailed guidelines on how to successfully interview legal professionals in such a way as to keep cultural and structural factors in mind.

Conclusion

This chapter delved into the methodological nuances of research into the viewpoints of Polish judges with regard to the part empathy plays in their decision-making. Identified and emphasized were the inherent challenges when studying empathy within the legal context and the complexities involved when trying to understand and discuss this specific concept with justices. Elucidated herein was the rationale for selecting IDIs as the primary research method—as well as the limitations inherent in such a choice. Importantly, we highlight the absence of an existing psychometric scale for judicial empathy; yet even if such a scale were to be developed, it would not completely address the pertinent challenges (e.g., empathy being an umbrella concept, judges' typical lack of self-reflection on their decision-making). Especially addressed here were characteristics of the sample cohort and its representativeness, recognizing the confines of this research project. Nonetheless, bearing in mind all the methodological limitations, it is important to recognize that this study represents the first systematic attempt to explore the perspectives of justices in Poland with respect to the role of empathy in their professional lives.

References

Bandes, Susan A. 2011. "Moral Imagination in Judging." *Washburn Law Review* 51: 1–24.

Bednarek, Grażyna A. 2014. *Polish vs. American Courtroom Discourse. Inquisitorial and Adversarial Procedures of Witness Examination in Criminal Trials.* London: Palgrave Macmillan.

Braun Virginia and Victoria Clarke. 2006. "Using Thematic Analysis in Psychology." *Qualitative Research in Psychology* 3: 77–101.

Čuroš, Peter. 2023. "Attack or Reform: Systemic Interventions in the Judiciary in Hungary, Poland, and Slovakia." *Oñati Socio-Legal Ser* 13(2): 626–658.

Dudek, Michał and Mateusz Stępień. 2021. *Courtroom Power Distance Dynamics.* Cham: Springer.

Gupta, Surabhi and William S. Harvey. 2022. "The Highs and Lows of Interviewing Legal Elites." *International Journal of Qualitative Methods* 21. https://doi.org/10.1177/16094069221078733

GUS. 2022. *Statistical Yearbook of the Republic of Poland.* Warsaw.

Handcock, Mark S. and Krista Gile. 2011. "Comment: On the Concept of Snowball Sampling." *Sociological Methodology* 41(1): 367–371. https://doi.org/10.1111/j.1467-9531.2011.01243.x

Howlett, Martin. 2022. "Looking at the 'Field' through a Zoom Lens: Methodological Reflections on Conducting Online Research During a Global Pandemic." *Qualitative Research* 22(3): 387–402.

Jaremba, Urszula and Elaine Mak. 2014. "Interviewing Judges in the Transnational Context." *Law and Method* 05.

Jullien, François. 2011. *The Silent Transformations.* London, New-York and Calcutta: Seagull.

Korkea-aho, Emilia and Päivi Leino. 2019. "Interviewing Lawyers: A Critical Self-Reflection on Expert Interviews as a Method of EU Legal Research." *European Journal of Legal Studies* 12: 17–47.

Lee, Ann F. 2017. *Interviewing in Social Science Research: A Relational Approach.* London: Routledge.

Mańko, Rafał. 2013. "Weeds in the Gardens of Justice? The Survival of Hyperpositivism in Polish Legal Culture as a Symptom/Sinthome." *Pólemos* 7(2): 207–233. https://doi.org/10.1515/pol-2013-0011

Maroney, Terry A. 2011. "The Persistent Cultural Script of Judicial Dispassion." *California Law Review* 99: 629–681.

Matthes, Claudia Y. 2022. "Judges as Activists: How Polish Judges Mobilise to Defend the Rule of Law." *East European Politics* 38(3): 468–487.

Merryman, John H. and Rogerio Pérez-Perdomo. 2018. *The Civil Law Tradition: An Introduction to the Legal Systems of Europe and Latin America*. Redwood City: Stanford University Press.
Mistygacz, Michał. 2020. "The Position of the Judge in Poland Within the Judicial System." *Studia Politologiczne* 58: 25–48.
Puleo, Leonardo and Ramona Coman. 2024. "Explaining Judges' Opposition When Judicial Independence is Undermined: Insights from Poland, Romania, and Hungary." *Democratization* 31(1): 47–69.
Ryan, Andrea. 2016. "Comparative Procedural Traditions: Poland's Journey from Socialist to 'Adversarial' System." *The International Journal of Evidence & Proof* 20(4): 305–325.
Sadurski, Wojciech. 2019. *Poland's Constitutional Breakdown*. Oxford: OUP.
Salmons, Janet E. 2014. *Doing Qualitative Research Online*. Thousand Oaks: Sage.
Stępień, Mateusz and Ewa Radomska. 2024. "Rethinking Hate Speech and Cyberhate Concepts: The Case of Smear Campaigns Against Judges in Poland." In *Handbook on Cyber Hate: Law and Visual Jurisprudence*, edited by Anne Wagner and Sarah Marusek. 191–213. Cham: Springer.
Szwed, Marcin. 2023. "Fixing the Problem of Unlawfully Appointed Judges in Poland in the Light of the ECHR." *Hague Journal on the Rule of Law* 15: 353–384.
Zoll, Fryderyk and Leah Wortham. 2019. "Judicial Independence and Accountability: Withstanding Political Stress in Poland." *Fordham International Law Journal* 42: 875–948.

3 Judges and the struggle to understand empathy

Mateusz Stępień

Initial thoughts and points of departure

As signaled in the Introduction, previous studies on judicial empathy have largely overlooked the perspectives of judges themselves and have neglected their understanding of empathy, perceptions of its role in judicial decision-making, and a recognition of its limitations and associated risks. This chapter addresses that gap, while Chapter 4 will build on this by exploring how judges envision empathy as it functions in the judicial setting. We aim to expand the discourse in stages by first looking at how judges conceptualize empathy and then examining how they perceive its application.

One particularly striking observation is the scarcity of research systematically mapping people's categorizations and conceptualizations of empathy. Furthermore, there is a notable lack of studies focusing on how specific groups perceive, understand, and conceptualize empathy from within. That deficiency highlights the need for research from the vantage point of those directly involved in its application, rather than from external sources, measures, or predefinitions.

Nonetheless, some studies have explored laypeople's notions about empathy. One exception is Judith Hall et al. (2021), who looked into how individuals define empathy and then categorized responses according to prevailing theoretical approaches. In Hall et al.'s (2021) study, participants were asked a general question about their definition of empathy, with responses analyzed in correspondence with frameworks dominant in the literature. Along similar lines, studies in the medical context—such as those by Sina Tavakol et al. (2012) or Joanna von Knorring et al. (2019)—have tracked definitions and perceptions.

But while providing valuable, albeit general, information, those research projects did not specifically focus on professional subsets of society. Additionally, the methodologies employed typically involved asking simple questions, lacking the complexity needed when exploring empathy in specific professional contexts and when digging into subtleties and points of tension between understandings. For our part, we not only asked judges to define empathy in open-ended terms but also looked at particular issues commonly

DOI: 10.4324/9781003546580-4

associated with it. This approach allowed us to delve deeper into the thoughts and opinions of judges, thereby providing a more nuanced understanding of their conceptualizations of empathy.

As touched on in Chapter 2, asking someone about empathy—especially regarding its usage in an explicit setting—constitutes a challenge from the start. Beyond problems already discussed, two other concerns warrant attention. First, it must be remembered that empathy carries positive connotations and is largely regarded as praiseworthy. However, there are voices arguing that empathy is a neutral capacity: It can be employed for prosocial, moral, and altruistic aims or, alternatively, for manipulation and the planning of immoral behaviors. This gives rise to potential strains: How do judges reconcile its pivotal role in social interactions outside the courtroom with perceived limits on its place in judicial decision-making? Where do judges draw the line against applying empathy, and why exactly there?

Second, it should also be considered that empathy has played a relatively marginal role in the way legal professionals approach their work. Empathy has not been long recognized as a component of the juridical professions. Indeed, it can be speculated that empathy's common association with emotions and affects has, at times, minimized recognition of its potentially constructive role in judicial decision-making. Moreover, for decades, there has been something of a silence about empathy. Rare or absent have been discussions about its flaws and dangers, or even attempts to defend judges from empathy's influence. Instead, the discourse has focused primarily on a broader range of factors (e.g., judges' emotions, worldviews, religious views), but not specifically on empathy. Only the debate sparked by then-President Barack Obama's statements (see Chapter 1) on empathy as a desirable trait in a nominee to the bench brought this issue to the fore for a while. But judicial milieux seem quiet about the subject—neither praising nor critiquing empathy in the law. Perhaps this arises out of a feeling that, if empathy is something positive and prosocial, then critiquing its role in judging might seem awkward. However—as we have maintained and as this book emphasizes—something is stirring with reference to the empathic sensitivities and abilities employed at work by justices—whether they are aware of it or not.

With all this in mind, while focusing on the judges' understanding of empathy, this chapter strives to answer a few key research questions. These include:

- What characteristics define judges' approach to empathy (e.g., can judges identify any limitations to empathy in general?)
- What are the registers of meanings associated with empathy employed by judges?
- Do judges blend empathy with compassion and morality, or do justices perceive these states as distinct?

By addressing these questions, a more comprehensive understanding of how judges perceive and interpret empathy will be gained. This exploration could facilitate broader discussions on how people conceptualize empathy and what they think of its nature; it will be helpful in understanding how judges see empathy in their work. Ultimately, this will help in distinguishing and comprehending the most basic strategies judges employ in their judicial labor.

Typologies of understanding empathy in the professional literature

The limits of this book preclude a survey of the diverse discussions across academic fields about how empathy is understood, but it is necessary to map the reservoir of meanings associated with this term in the scholarly literature. This mapping will be crucial to interpreting how judges think about empathy: Their perspectives must be contextualized against the backdrop of prevailing tendencies and the range of possibilities. Although meta-studies on definitions of empathy—such as the works by Benjamin Cuff et al. (2016) or Michaela Guthridge and Melita Giummarra (2021)—provide useful lenses through which to look at all this, the following discussion will be based on typologies of how empathy is understood. The intention is not to engage in a detailed study of each and every definitional possibility, but rather to provide a framework within which to contextualize views expressed by judges. By referring to these typologies, we can analyze and evaluate their understandings of empathy without being confined to a single definitional path. This approach will facilitate a grasp of two opposite ways of thinking about empathy that goes beyond simple differentiation between the cognitive and affective.

First, regarding the definition's scope, empathy can be categorized as either narrow or broad, seen as a delimited concept concentrated on a singular process, or as a broad umbrella term encompassing various, often discrete, processes. Some definitions may consist of a single element (e.g., Jordan et al. 2016), while others constitute a wide-ranging list (e.g., Davis 1983; Carré et al. 2013). Single-item conceptualizations are found in the literature of the field, but the view that empathy should be treated as an encompassing conception is becoming more popular, leading to distinctions made between its components or factors. Moving away from reducing empathy to an uncontrollable reaction to external stimuli and toward multiprocess definitions sheds a brighter light on the complexity of the term.

Second, with reference to the types of processes involved, the literature distinguishes between the affective and cognitive. Affective empathy evokes an emotional resonance—mimicking emotional states or feeling someone else's emotions (e.g., Maibom 2017). In contrast, cognitive empathy looks at nonaffective processes such as perspective-taking—recognizing and understanding another's experience, or communicating and confirming that understanding with the other person (e.g., Spaulding 2017). Nonetheless, it is important to note that the affective/cognitive divide is based on an imperfect, Cartesian understanding of the human mind, and some scholars are deliberately shunning the distinction.

Third, approaches also vary according to the assumed duration of the empathizing: momentary or continuous (see Batson 2009). Sometimes it is perceived as a fleeting state or act, lasting only as long as the nature of the empathic state or stimulus allows. At other times, under certain conditions, empathy is perceived as a stable personality trait, a pervasive filter or attitude shaping the overall behavior and decisions of the empathizer. For example, Eric Leake (2023: 42) notes that "empathy is realized not only in moments but also in orientations as ways of approaching." In this vein, some argue that empathy is a virtue (see Battaly 2011; Stępień 2025).

Fourth is the low versus high control distinction. Low control over empathizing—associated with little conscious thought—leads to automatic reactions. Conversely, high control is seen as a motivated reaction: Internal prompts lead individuals to actively engage empathetically (Zaki 2014). Little to no control over empathic responses may result in biased, automatic conclusions often drawn without proper inference, while approaches that emphasize high control see it as enabling deliberate navigation of empathic impulses. Prolonged development of control allows for more thoughtful and balanced responses; hence high control approaches advocate for intentional and mindful engagement with empathy, suggesting that individuals can train themselves to harness and direct their empathic reactions in more constructive and appropriate ways.

Fifth, approaches differ with regard to the target of empathic acts: There are ways of comprehending empathy that are centered intra-personally and others centered extra-personally. Empathy-like abilities typically mean to enter into the psychological state of others, such as their emotions, feelings, sensations, and ways of thinking. However, an alternative approach suggests using empathic abilities to understand the wider situations in which individuals find themselves. This entails more than just episodic or stable processes and includes the social status of a given person. In this regard, Elizabeth Segal (2018: 4) proposed the notion of social empathy, understood as "the ability to understand people and other social groups by perceiving and experiencing their life situations. To do so involves learning about and understanding the historical context of group experiences, including the structural inequalities that have shaped communities." That line of thinking brings contextual understanding and macro perspective-taking, which differs significantly from the mere gaining of insight into someone's mind (Segal 2018: 15).

The sixth and final perspective on this pertains to diverging viewpoints about the necessity of outwardly manifesting empathy. While some contend that such expressions are superfluous, others assert that those expressions are of fundamental import. Conventional definitions centering on internal processes suggest that empathy can exist without overt external displays. Conversely, alternative perspectives argue that outward manifestations are indispensable and emphasize the manifestation of verbal and nonverbal behavior in a genuine empathic act. For instance, Melissa Fuller et al. (2023: 169) characterize empathy as "the willingness and ability to understand other persons' perspectives, beliefs, and emotions and to confirm and express this understanding in communicative behavior."

These six categorization criteria provide the cornerstones for two contrasting, large-scale models of understanding empathy. More meaningfully, the six sets of opposites align with the distinction between both low and high empathy, which includes these differentiations to some extent (Camassa 2024: 31–55), and between easy and difficult empathy (Leake 2023: 18–64).

Of the two contrasting models, the first is characterized by a narrow range, covering primarily affective processes and focusing on momentary duration, low control, a person-centered focus, and a lack of emphasis on outward manifestations. This could also be labeled easy empathy, which has its limitations: associated biases can lead to suboptimal and even undesirable outcomes. Among the most researched empathy biases are the familiarity bias (a tendency to empathize more with those we know), similarity bias (a tendency to empathize more with those with whom we share some traits), and the presence or here-and-now bias (a tendency to empathize more with those who are present versus those who are absent). However, those same inherent characteristics of easy empathy do have some positive impact, as they provide bridges to others' experiences.

In comparison, the second model of difficult empathy enfolds a full spectrum of items associated with cognitive or cognitive-affective processes, continuous duration, high control, a focus extending beyond the individual to include external circumstances, and often, but not necessarily, emphasizes the manifestation of certain behaviors and expressions. This model makes certain demands of the empathizer, requiring effort, monitoring, and navigation. Key is that easy empathy can be transformed or, more accurately, developed into difficult empathy (Stępień 2025).

These two divergent models—encapsulating six categories of differences in how empathy is understood in the literature—manifest contrasting propensities with respect to the basics, range, and qualities of empathy. Again, at first glance, easy empathy seems more worrying in a judicial context due to its potential biases and lack of control. Analogously, difficult empathy—with its stress on cognitive processes, high control, and possible hindrance of outward manifestations—appears less likely to undermine fundamental judicial values such as impartiality and objectivity.

A general outline of judges' views

Summarizing how judges comprehend empathy and their views on its relationship to compassion and morality is an ambitious mission because the term is ambiguous and can be taken in diverse ways. Additionally, the richness of the themes and views presented by the judges with whom we conversed adds to the complexity. While the interviewees did their best, many faced difficulties in grappling with empathy and associated issues, as they are neither trained nor accustomed to reflecting upon this matter. Given that judges are likely without training in psychology or philosophy, nuanced differences might escape detection. Nevertheless, a rough outline of these judges' stances on empathy can be sketched.

First, in the initial observation, certain judges expressed a well-structured, cohesive, and intellectually stimulating approach to empathy. These individuals engaged in reflective discussions informed by diverse sources such as literature or personal experience. Those experiences included therapeutic interventions centered precisely on emotional explorations, or extensive professional careers during which these judges dealt with the complexities of empathy in human lives and in the judicial domain. The explications regarding empathy provided by these individuals evidenced a profound level of introspection and a dedication to exploring its weightier inferences for their professional and personal lives. These judges avoided simplistic interpretations, wrestling instead with the intricacies; they recognized the challenges, constraints, and subtleties inherent in grasping empathy. Many of their insights resonated with the most profound observations in the specialized literature. By comparison, the expositions we heard from other judges seemed superficial, lacked in-depth awareness, and were weakly substantiated. Such outlooks appeared to conform more to prevailing professional norms, rather than display a healthy skepticism.

Instead of classifying our cohort of judges into distinct subgroups but still considering the existence of both types within the sample, we present here a particularly sophisticated opinion. Illustrating a mature approach to the concept, a civil judge [32] whose interests extend beyond the law defined empathy as "a mode of feeling together and an ability to take on the perspective of another person." This definition encapsulates processes akin to emotional contagion and was vividly illustrated by the judge through the example of a friend who could feel others' pain and through his own perspective-taking in which the judge excelled. When asked to explain the relationship between the two levels of empathy, the judge described feeling together as an instinct, likening it to how children react intensely to others' pain or joy. Nevertheless, perceiving from the perspective of another person involves more than an instinctive reaction: There must be imagination, experience, awareness, openness, and the ability to somewhat detach oneself emotionally. This judge emphasized the importance of self-reflexivity when entering the position of another. In some sense, the judge also drew the distinction between easy and difficult empathy, demonstrating a nuanced recognition of issues with empathy in the execution of a judge's professional duties.

Second, it should be noted that, at the beginning of the interview, the judges were prompted to discuss empathy in general, without reference to the judicial context. Nonetheless, several interviewees quickly opened with discussions of their role as judges, suggesting a preference for deliberations on familiar territory [8, 9, 10, 11, 26, 34, 35, 36]. Further, for some judges [1, 3, 20, 37], it was clearly easier to engage with the topic in the context in which they customarily dealt with it. For example, one judge [8] directly invoked the courtroom, referring to empathy as the ability to understand the perspective of those who approach him with problems. Likewise, one judge [36] equated empathy with "getting into the role" of the party involved in the case, while another [34], after presenting empathy as sensitivity, provided examples arising from a courthouse context, such as being tolerant of someone's mistakes. Additionally, while discussing her definition, another judge [35] accentuated the importance of communicating the motives behind the final verdict to the parties involved. Still another judge [10], clearly referencing judicial settings, characterized empathy as understanding, but not necessarily experiencing, the condition of the other side, asserting that empathy contributes to being a good judge. This tendency to situate discussions of the concept in the courthouse likely reflects a higher level of comfort when on familiar territory dealing with concrete cases, not abstract notions.

A third significant observation is that most judges provided very broad strokes and even overinclusive characterizations of empathy; nearly all the definitions were multifactorial (see Hall et al. 2021). Over the course of the interview, several judges would expand on their original description and associate empathy with additional qualities. To some extent, this was a result of the natural flow of conversation during which newly presented follow-ups inspired our interviewees to clarify or modify their explication. In other instances, the reach of a definition expanded during an interview due to the fact that judges do not typically contemplate the meaning of empathy in extenso. Consequently, when asked about it during the conversation, they naturally explored their own intuitions and thoughts, sharing common associations and personal perspectives.

While many examples of judges' multifactorial understandings of empathy could be discussed, one example is especially emblematic. A family judge [27] presented one of the most densely packed definitions, rich with meanings often treated separately in the literature. For this judge, empathy is "a feature, a quality, which enables getting into, understanding the situation, [understanding] what they feel, . . . think in some way. [It's] also connected with what we [sic] would call kindness, respect for the other person, but on another level. . . . Generally, [it's] related to understanding and a kind of compassion." Here, a variety of processes can be identified: getting inside someone's skin, understanding, kindness, respect, compassion, and so on. Asked about the main features of an empathic person, this judge pointed out the importance of being careful when dealing with people and to consider the impact of one's actions—whether this might "hurt, harm the other person." This was also an interview in which a follow-up question brought out an interesting point.

The fourth finding is that all the interviewees made a distinction between empathy and compassion (see, e.g., Davis 2017). However, their comprehensions of each of these two concepts varied (as it is in the specialized literature; see Goetz, Simon-Thomas 2017), and so did their perspectives on the relationships between the two. Though we are only outlining the general approach taken by our interviewees, two motifs on the distinction between empathy and compassion surfaced and deserve a closer look. Later we will see other opinions on empathy versus compassion that did not always translate with such clarity in the judicial context.

One motif could be called affectivity: For a considerable number of judges, the distinction between empathy and compassion lies primarily in the affective or nonaffective nature of the concept. For instance, a judge [18, likewise 21] portrayed empathy as the opposite of compassion, describing the former as an ability to read and comprehend the emotions of others. He insisted that one can empathize only in a "solely intellectual way," and the intellect can be trained to read emotions. In a similar vein, another judge [2] perceived compassion as a type of emotion, while empathy was seen as a skill. On the one hand, he emphasized this fundamental difference, but, on the other, this judge also identified certain connections between the two, noting that "empathy can lead to compassion." Similarly, another judge [6, likewise 17, 34] described compassion as a "more emotion-related concept . . . [which] does not necessarily mean understanding." This substantiated his opinion that empathy is not related to emotion, and therefore its role in the judicial context is more legitimate. According to another view [10], compassion is seen as a simple, emotionally loaded encounter, whereas empathy transcends mere reaction to another's misfortune. Often, the perceived difference between these two lies in the fact that empathy aims at understanding, which is not the case for compassion. One of the judges [22] observed that, colloquially, empathy is often erroneously conflated with compassion. In the case of the former, however (in both the cognitive and emotional sense), the crux lies in "understanding [others'] emotions and how they perceive the world . . . the ability to see the world from their point of view." Another judge [3] distinguishing between empathy and compassion tended to associate the latter with a "feeling when seeing another person [in pain, traumatic condition, etc.]," which is distant from "an attempt to understand the feelings of the other person." Moreover, for some interviewees [e.g. 8], the strong emotional nature of compassion is related to the fact that it relies on feeling the same thing as the receiver of compassion. Another judge [15] stressed that "compassion is related to taking upon oneself another's emotion, co-feeling the same thing, and empathy is some kind of understanding their state but without getting into [someone]." Thus, compassion is pictured as an affective state, while empathy as more nonaffective, not requiring emotional identification with a target individual.

The second motif deals with empathy seen as much more than a (momentary) feeling of pity associated with compassion. For a considerable group of judges, compassion is seen as a more prompt and flattering reaction than empathy. This indicates that empathy is perceived as more stable and controllable (closer to difficult empathy). A common thread running through the interviews was compassion as ephemeral, lacking permanence and solidity. From a viewpoint that could be representative of the popular way of grasping compassion, "it demands less . . . one can stop and not move to the stage of empathy" [9]. This suggests that empathy covers much more than compassion, understood as feeling pity at the sight of another's misfortune. Quite similar was a view expressed by other judges, for whom "compassion is close to feeling pity, lamentation," while empathy covers much more since it leads to "understanding" [11] and "feeling the other's feelings" [35]. In this sense, "empathy is deeper than compassion" [7]. In the same vein, another interviewee [20] stated that "compassion is related to feeling sorry [for someone], and in the case of empathy, one wants to cooperate [with others]." Empathy is more oriented at a social praxis and not solely a cognitive state, not reduced to triggered emotions.

Empathy is a fuller process than compassion and calls for—as one judge mentioned [23]—"participation in good and bad feelings, thus I understand someone's emotions," whereas compassion is thinner though possibly leading to "support and comfort [for someone] in distress." Another judge [14] saw empathy as a general, human-centered attitude involving openness and cooperativeness; she felt it leads to attempts to resolve a problem vis-à-vis momentarily feeling something (like compassion) that could not translate into assistance and solutions. This link between empathy and "helping" is stressed by others [32] as well. Another justice [16] mentioned that "compassion does not bring anything, as this is a one-sided type of relation." In contrast, empathy does much more and involves social relations. Summing up this strand, empathizing generally requires more time and effort, whereas the feeling of compassion is much narrower in time and, in some sense, a simpler act.

It is intriguing to consider whether distinctions between empathy and compassion made by legal professionals arise from an underlying intuition or established belief that compassion poses a threat to the decision-making process. It is possible that a tendency to view empathy as more acceptable and easier to defend is linked to a perception of compassion as potentially problematic due to its association with emotionality and its professedly uncontrollable nature. Compassion could give rise to concerns about impartiality and objectivity in legal judgments: It is typically directed toward persons in distress and engages a heartfelt response to that distress, regardless of whether the individual has actually shared their emotions.

Returning to the general sketch of the views emerging from the interviews, a fifth observation is that judges encountered significant difficulties when addressing correlations between empathy and morality, as explicitly mentioned by several of them [8, 28, 37]. The problem likely stems from the inherent complexity of the subject matter, compounded by the diverse ways in which individuals conceptualize morality and its connection to empathy. The nature of morality itself can be very elusive and contentious, with diverse philosophical perspectives offering contrasting frameworks for understanding moral rules and principles (not to mention ethics). Moreover, attempts to conjoin morality and empathy introduce additional layers of density as, predictably, these two concepts can interact in multiple possible ways. For some judges, dealing with these questions may have proven challenging due to a lack of clarity or consensus regarding their own personal beliefs or understanding of morality vis-à-vis empathy. Additionally, morality's interdisciplinarity—drawing from philosophy, psychology, and sociology—may have presented further obstacles for justices in Poland whose education is tightly centered on the law, legal reasoning, and decision-making. Overall, the difficulties encountered by our group of judges underscore the intricate nature of these concepts and a need for careful consideration and exploration when examining their interplay.

The perspectives of our interviewees were much more varied on the empathy-morality relationship than the empathy-compassion one. As with the latter, for the purposes of our outlined sketch, we again identified the key themes that surfaced. For several judges, a number of linkages do exist between empathy and morality, but some justices acknowledge a connection without delving into any specifics [12, 19, 33]. However, in accord with what could be called a correlation thesis, one family judge [21] asserted that being empathetic and being moral go hand in hand: "It is hard for me to imagine that someone is immoral and empathic." Buttressing that, another family judge [23, also 29] pointed out that "people who are moral are capable of being more empathetic." Another perspective [6] suggested that "understanding other humans [via empathy] allows for a different attitude toward them, which is not subjective-like, for example . . . and this is an element of a morality-based approach." One judge [16], equating empathy with openness, admitted that she treats "the imperative to be open" as a moral principle, emphasizing her commitment to cultivating an open attitude. Empathy is seen here as an instance of morality in general, understood differently than a set of norms.

But other perspectives also emerged from the sample. One judge [11] even highlighted the relationship between these two concepts, asserting that the moral principle "do unto others as you would have them do unto you" implies an innate need for empathy. In her eyes, empathy involves grasping what is pleasant or favorable for others, which, in turn, necessitates a form of perspective-taking. While the link between empathy and some variation of the Golden Rule was not uncommon in the interviews, the version she offered involves social actors voluntarily restraining themselves as they project their own mindset onto others. The Golden Rule also appeared in an interesting response from another judge [2], who differentiated between morality as a set of specific norms and morality identified with the Golden Rule. Aligning with the literature, this judge acknowledged that empathy is closely related to morality, but not morality as a set of norms. Although not including the senses usually associated with empathy, this refined distinction was unique among those in our sample.

Only one judge [24] dove into the stronger, more vital nature of empathy in this vein, echoing Martin Hoffman's thesis (2000) with an avowal that "empathy is basic for understanding moral norms—a lot of principles have a basis in empathy." However, for several judges [more explicitly 4, 10, 18], there are no robust connections between empathy and morality. Some, however, acknowledging the problematic nature of this issue, held on to a distinction between them [3]. Stressing the difference, one judge [5] saw empathy as a "more intricate skill." A family judge [20] stressed that everyone possesses a moral code sharing something of a relationship with empathy, but suggesting finally that both spheres work somewhat autonomously, "there could be an empathic act that contradicts what morality demands."

Dominant ways of understanding empathy by judges

The ways judges in our sample defined empathy can be segregated into several categories, shedding more light onto various stances, directions, choices, and tensions found in their interview responses. Our classification will serve not only as an interesting exploration of views on the nature of empathy itself, but also facilitate such investigations within the judicial sphere.

Perspective-taking

When looking at empathy as a taking on of the perspective of others, the associated cluster of meanings refers to a range of processes—such as seeing the situation through another person's glasses or putting oneself in the shoes of another. Because empathy is multifaceted, such threads extracted from the transcripts are often tangled with other meanings.

Some judges directly employed the perspective-taking approach to empathy. For instance, one judge [2, likewise 19] understood empathy nearly exactly as described earlier: an "ability to put oneself in the place of the other person, seeing things from their eyes; an attempt to understand what they can feel in a given moment, how they could perceive a given situation." Similarly, another interviewee [17] described empathy via the perspective-taking lens but cautioned how empathizers put themselves into another's "position and their life situation." A few judges accentuated the "walking a mile in someone's shoes" understanding with respect to momentary, emergency cases; other judges focused on a more loose and sweeping understanding such as entering into a set of life circumstances. Nevertheless, both standpoints are instructive because they illustrate an "I-centered" perspective-taking ("how would I feel in this same situation"), rather than an "other-centered" one. Interestingly, in these examples, the judges declared that the target of empathic behavior is a broader situation, not narrowly defined cognitive states. This shows that empathy as perspective-taking differs from a "theory of mind" or simply reading another's state of mind. Moreover, it seems that, following this line of thinking, understanding is the ultimate aim of empathy, and putting oneself into someone else's shoes functions as a means.

Another judge [21] concisely defined empathy as "understanding other humans," but later clarified that "it is related to life experiences. If we experienced something ourselves, we are capable of relating this to that and eventually putting oneself into the situation of another human." Later in the interview, however, this judge once more equated empathy with "entering into their situation." However, this justice did not recognize the potential dangers of establishing a link between the capability of grasping another person's situation and the possession of certain personal experiences. After all, the universe of one's private experiences delimits when and how (even weak) perspective-taking can be realized effectively. Key, therefore, is self-awareness that facilitates recognition of one's own possible limits and biases. This leads to a question about whether selective perspective-taking could underpin easy empathy in cases where one's own experiences (being incomplete and idiosyncratic) are involved. Interestingly, very seldom did our interviewees dwell on the putatively negative effect of referring to their personal experiences during a trial. Fortuitously, this issue was picked up by one judge [35], who saw empathy as "putting oneself, getting into the role of this other person, and seeing how they perceive this." The judge added that "we are built by our own experiences; however, this person need not have had the same [experiences]." Here empathy was pictured as an attempt to see the world as others do, but precisely in order to transcend one's own experiences and therefore come to a decision without (or with minimal) prejudice.

A more complex and multifactorial understanding was presented by a family judge [15], who described empathy as "embodying someone else's way of thinking, delving into their emotional states and reasoning." She succinctly summarized the key point by equating empathy with the "ability to look at reality through someone else's eyes" and gaining insight into "what [the other] can experience in a given moment"—something closely aligned with the concept of perspective-taking. The judge, however, added a subtle layer, noting that empathy is "sometimes perhaps the ability to identify with the states of this person." This introduced a unique dimension to empathy not found elsewhere in the sample. Her approach also addressed other-centered perspective-taking, as well as the tensions between automatic empathizing and processes driven by the "control of reason, to stop at a given moment and try to look at the world through the eyes of another person." Thus, this family judge explored differences between low- and high-control approaches to empathy.

Interestingly, in one case, the perspective-taking view on empathy was linked to a specific version of the Golden Rule. A judge [9], in presenting his understanding of empathy, shared an important message his father had relayed to him when he, as a young boy, harmed others: "Put yourself in the situation of the person you hurt." Consequently, the judge saw empathy as "entering into the situation of another person" in order to understand how that individual feels.

Something important was noticeable in the words of another judge [28], who began with an overall description of empathy as a way of perceiving another person by "putting oneself into the place of a given person." Although this appeared to be a typical perspective-taking approach, this woman added (after a few follow-up questions) "feeling someone's emotions" as a feature. This blurs the boundaries between these two meanings, but it also suggests how deeply ingrained is a combination, among Polish judges, of multifactorial thinking about empathy alongside feeling together as its key feature.

Getting into (emotionally entering into)

Judges frequently described empathy as a form of *wczucie się*. According to the canonical *Dictionary of the Polish Language* (*Słownik Języka Polskiego*), that reflexive verb means "to experience the same feeling as someone else and thus understand someone else's condition," as well as "penetrating deeply into something, getting to know and understand it." The first definition suggests a strong emotional connection, while the second accents a deeper understanding without necessarily involving strong emotional identification. However, the fundamental meaning of the verb revolves around "feeling" and "sensing." "Getting [feeling] into" closely resembles the German *Einfühlung*, which translates to "feeling into" or, more precisely, "entering emotionally into"; in English, it connotes a "getting into" a theatrical or other role. Crucial for our analyses was to delineate how the judges in our sample interpreted and applied this verb in presenting empathy as *wczucie się*.

For example, one judge [33] understood this getting-into approach as "an ability to get into the needs and situation of another person, as well as the being, that is, an animal." This perspective highlights that empathy extends not only to humans but also to other living creatures. Additionally, it emphasizes the role of empathy in discerning or reconstructing its recipient's needs. However, those needs are shrouded somewhat by ambiguity: Does it refer to subjective or objectified needs as uncovered by the empathizer? Here, the getting-into approach suggests a broader and deeper process than merely entering the emotional state of the other: It targets the needs and the situation in which the other living creature finds itself. Certainly, this is more than just getting into someone's emotions.

In a somewhat similar vein, another judge [3] characterized empathy as "understanding the needs and feelings of the other side . . . looking at the other human, not through the prism of one's own ego, but to understand and get into (*wczuć się*) the situation of the human on the other side." This definition underscores getting into as one of several means of understanding another person. But the target here is "the situation," which calls for details: Does getting into the situation mean an attempt to comprehend someone else's momentary or stable thoughts and perspectives based on a broader context?

Another judge [12] proposed a two-element view on empathy as "a skill, ability to read the others' emotions, emotional states, and the skill of getting into them, understanding them." This approach is narrower, as it focuses solely on understanding someone's emotions. However, there's a question about the relationship between reading others' emotions and getting into them and whether the former is a precursor to the latter.

One judge [29] presented an understanding of empathy and its role, describing it as "getting into, or an attempt to get into the emotions, but also the feelings of another human we are dealing with, . . . in order to better understand them, better communicate with and act [with them]." This judge highlighted the communication aspect of empathy, emphasizing not only the understanding of emotions but also the reasons underlying such a task. Interestingly, this is another version of the "getting into" way of grasping empathy. The courtroom context slightly surfaces from this statement, as the justice emphasized the importance of not being judgmental and remaining open to understanding the other party's perspective. Summing this up, the getting-into paradigm is not uniform and does not solely focus on emotional processes.

Co-feeling (co-feeling together)

When describing empathy, a significant number of judges referred to the Polish term *współodczuwanie* (a gerund noun), a challenging term to translate. Again, referring to the *Dictionary of the Polish Language* (*Słownik Języka Polskiego*) cited earlier, *współodczuwać* (as a verb) means "co-feeling" or "feeling with"—in the sense of *com*passion or *com*miseration, but without the element of pity. It is further associated with "getting into someone else's feelings," closely aligned with the concept described earlier as "getting into." For instance, one judge [5] explained "co-feeling" as "getting into, entering emotionally into." When translating *współodczuwanie* into English, one must focus on the first syllable, *współ*, which means "co(m)-" or "together," and the second part of the word that points to "feeling," "experiencing," or "sensing," but always with an affective tone. Thus, this literary term encapsulates a state of "co-feeling" together or feeling with: one person endeavoring to directly sense what another feels. This process is undoubtedly emotional or, at the very least, emotionally charged.

For example, a judge [4] defined empathy as "co-feeling, that is getting into the situation of another person, at least the attempt to do so, as, frankly, we can never state and feel what the other person feels, and at least an attempt to take into account their situation, their feelings." This judge used strongly affective language, but the object of the co-feeling is not the person, but rather the situation—a motif pinpointed with regard to extra-mind-centered approaches to empathy. Another interviewee [5] said: "I identify [empathize] with co-feeling . . . with such an understanding of the feeling of someone's emotions . . . the ability to get into these emotions." Here, the other's emotions are at the heart of empathizing.

At times judges initiated their descriptions of empathy by accenting co-feeling and then adding the perspective-taking component. For instance, some equated empathy with "a skill to co-feel others' situation, and understanding their situation—looking a little at the case from their eyes" [11] and/or viewing it as "a form of co-feeling and an ability to take the perspective of another person" [32]. The co-feeling is accompanied here by other elements falling under the swelling umbrella of empathy. In a similar vein, another judge [13] began answering the question about his understanding of empathy by stating that it is a co-feeling, subsequently inclusive of an "ability to get into the situation of another human, an attempt to understand their emotions, sensations." Later the judge mentioned the benefits of empathy in social life (e.g., better understanding of motivations, better communication). Asked for more detail, he mentioned an "ability to listen to a person; to create such an impression." Importantly, good listening skills were rarely mentioned in parts of the interviews when general empathy was being discussed. Moreover, empathy was not pictured as a momentary flash, but as an element in the management of social relations where creating an impression is essential. It should be noticed that this last judge distinguished between understanding and justifying someone (clearly referencing the judicial context).

One judge [23] offered a less coherent approach to empathy. She started by describing it as co-feeling, which is not unusual considering the concept's emotional connotations. However, after this characteristic, the judge stated: "I know that it could be tricky to perceive empathy as feeling the same thing as someone else [feels], so I am very careful and treat empathy as a situation in which I could understand someone's feelings, but do not feel them as mine." A slight inconsistency manifested itself in the fact that she initially mentioned co-feeling, but later delimited empathy to an understanding of feelings, but not feelings themselves. Perhaps her judicial role played a part in this, as the judge subconsciously realized the impact of co-feeling in the judicial realm.

This leads to an important issue: In general, do judges who view empathy as centered around co-feeling think about the literal sense of *współodczuwanie*, a word that implies everyday emotions and some sort of sharing? Her subsequent remarks during the interview provided certain clues on how to read this. She mirrored others' emotional states (e.g., someone's sadness resulted in her being sad), but later "the differentiation, demarcation—between this understanding of others' feelings and one's feelings—came." Thus, co-feeling is just a stage in an extended developmental process—one obviously harder to explain and articulate.

As our final example in this section, a judge [18] defined empathy as "an ability to recognize others' emotions and understand these emotions, thus co-sharing these emotions which other humans possess . . . entering into their emotional situation, and maybe also an intellectual motivation [to do so]." The accent of empathic competencies was on the emotions of others—not only reading those emotions but also sharing them. Later during the conversation, the judge clarified: "I am talking about empathy in the emotional sense as co-feeling."

General open-minded approach

Perhaps the approach to empathy that focuses on open-mindedness does not represent typical ideas about this topic as found in the specialized literature, but several judges nonetheless explored this avenue. Often, this theme has been accompanied by more traditional ways of thinking about empathy.

One judge [6] spoke about it as "understanding the situation of the other person," expanding this to "getting into and understanding the situation of the other human." Later, the interviewee stressed that this delving into someone is especially needed in situations in which he "does not support [something], does not accept [something]." Just "then I try to understand the motivation, situation [of those with whom I do not agree]." Here, empathy is something motivated, something that works in deliberately transcending one's own perspective, strongly held views, predetermined decisions, etc. This is strongly embedded in the judicial context. Interestingly, this judge stressed that empathy is a more reason-related skill and a motivated one, "so I can try to impose on myself the attempt to understand someone." In this sense, empathy is also controllable and a competency that can be honed in order to preserve some sort of open-mindedness.

Another judge [7] characterized empathy as "understanding what another human feels or experiences [*przeżywa*]," which differs from the previously mentioned view, as it focuses on gaining access to the emotional and affective world of an individual. However, during the interview, this man clarified that empathy serves as a way to "not issue fast, cheap, and superficial judgments [*osądy*]." An empathic person, according to this perspective, refrains from making quick assessments and, instead, considers the context of a given behavior, which could subsequently alter assessment of that behavior. Context is deemed crucial in fully understanding a situation, suggesting that empathy helps judges avoid haste and bias.

This change in tone in the responses we heard highlights the dynamic nature of discussions about topics as complex as empathy. The line of questioning taken—that is, focusing on the features of an empathic person rather than on the meaning of empathy itself—could significantly enrich (as was often the case) or even alter the tenor of the answers given. Such a shift in tone was evident in the standpoint of another judge [4] who explained that her definition rested on "getting into"—a linking of empathy with "hearing this other person after providing some assessments regarding this person, . . . a willingness to listen, . . . a person who listens most of all."

Another judge [16] who extended the human-centered approach to the bench also proposed an understanding of empathy as being "open to other humans, to their situation, way of thinking, their way of seeing the situations." Unfortunately, these were only glimpses, and we do not know what openness really meant for the judge or what particular features form general openness as a trait. This could be a matter of avoiding judgmentalism, but also a lack of assumptions and prejudices. Interestingly, this thread was touched on by another interviewee [25] who saw empathy as "openness to other humans . . . interest in other persons, their, in some sense, interests broadly understood." This judge substantiated his view by referring to his religious background (Roman Catholicism), which teaches that "we are not living for oneself." Many depend on what the category of "openness" covers. Here empathy is a kind of general attitude, a filter on personality.

Varia

The clusters of meanings presented earlier do not encompass all the ways that judges in contemporary Poland understand empathy. Some approaches deviate considerably from the majority opinion, shifting away from typical ways of comprehending the concept.

First, in a human-centered approach, empathy is seen as a broad disposition encompassing several specific qualities. One judge [14] described empathy as "being open to other human [beings], understanding what triggers them, discerning their needs, attempting to get into their situation . . . comprehending the mechanisms that guide them . . . finding a path to agreement, and perhaps offering assistance—this entails seeing [deeper], as well as not being easily offended." This portrayal of empathy stresses cooperation, assistance, and understanding, while also distinguishing between understanding and justifying—something quite crucial in the judicial sphere. A humanistic approach was also explored by a criminal judge [1], who viewed empathy as a "sense of service for other humans . . . emerging from respect for other humans." This represented an idealized and atypical perspective on empathy, especially considering the judicial domain. Similarly, another judge [37] presented a general understanding of empathy as "tactful conduct in the broadest meaning of the word, depending on the situation, conditions . . . and being patient," covering a polite, adequate, sensitive approach toward others.

Second, imagining and mimicking were a less common theme in the judges' responses, with only a few references to these motives. One judge [30] equated empathy with "the possibility of imagining feelings, sensing what the other human experiences in the emotional sphere," while another described empathy as "mimicking other feelings" [15], highlighting the affective aspect of empathy.

Third, sensitivity was mentioned by but a few judges as a core aspect of empathy. Only a single judge [34] defined this as a "sensitiveness toward other humans, . . . lack of egoism, . . . having in mind the well-being of others . . . open to the needs of people." Last but not least, the fourth motif among the judges defined empathy as a process of understanding another person, aimed at different objects, such as the situation, person, or position. For example, one judge [10] described empathy as "understanding the situation of the other side, but not feeling the situation of others," even emphasizing the understanding aspect while maintaining a certain distance. Another judge [20] presented empathy as a "willingness to understand another person, a willingness to cooperate, collaborate with another person," portraying it as a cooperative attitude grounded in understanding. Overall, the understandings of empathy we gained from interviews with justices vary widely, encompassing a range of perspectives that reflect their individual views and experiences.

Conclusions

Judges' views on empathy widely differ, although some common threads can be detected in their expressed thoughts. According to our findings, a) judges differ in the sophistication of their thinking about empathy; b) judges often prefer to discuss empathy in the familiar context of the judiciary without directly addressing its limitations; c) judges distinguish between empathy and compassion, which is a positive as well as rather surprising; and d) they see the difficult relations between empathy and morality without assuming any simple relationships between them. In relation to the registers of meanings associated with empathy placed into action by judges, there is variability, which should be interpreted from the perspective of the umbrella-like approach to empathy. Keeping this in mind, the sample yielded the following approaches to empathy: a) perspective-taking, b) getting into, c) feeling together, d) open-mindedness, and e) a variety of miscellaneous approaches. The majority of the understandings presented herein have generally followed what the literature proposes, although some inconsistencies and over-inclusivity can be traced. Interestingly, several approaches stress that empathy is about grasping the other's situation or needs, and thus an extra-mind-centered approach is extensively expressed. Notably, certain judges accentuated empathy's emotional aspect, viewing it as a deep connection to the feelings and experiences of others. On the one hand, this emotional resonance is seen as integral to empathy, enabling individuals to truly understand and share in the emotions of others. On the other hand, some judges emphasize empathy as a cognitive process, focusing on understanding others' situations and perspectives, without necessarily sharing their emotions. For them, empathy involves active listening, sensitivity, and a willingness to see things from another's point of view. Interestingly, a few judges introduce unique perspectives, such as viewing empathy as a sense of service or a cooperative attitude toward achieving common goals. All these interpretations taken together highlight empathy's role, not only in understanding others but also in fostering collaboration and mutual respect.

Besides the previously described combinations of different factors or elements that are at least differentiated in the specialized literature, the next important observation is that one can distill the prevailing structure of judges' thinking about empathy. First, there is a mechanism—the process or processes which are the material substrates of the "empathic acts." This entails "getting into," "putting oneself in another's situation," or "imagining the other's position." No clues are provided, however, as to how empathic processes (e.g., getting into someone's emotions) actually happen and by which avenues they are achieved and whether they are limited to the given moment or cover longer internal actions. The judges almost never mentioned communication, demonstrating that someone is listening to and concerned about the other person. Nonverbal cues and the feedback factor convey that one party wants to understand the ideas and feelings of both sides nonjudgmentally and helpfully, and yet these were off the judges' radar. This signals problems with thinking about empathy in more interactional terms. Second is the target of these processes—which could be emotions, feelings, thoughts, ways of thinking, ways of perceiving the world, and reasons but also situations, positions, or location. The chosen target changes a lot and makes the whole emphasizing considerably different. The final component is the result of processes aimed at specific targets. These results may be desired but also, inevitably, "generated by empathic acts." This could lead to a deeper and broader understanding, enhanced communication, and/or epistemological change in the empathizer (e.g., debiasing, open-mindedness, or enhanced well-being for those experiencing empathy). Most approaches do not refer to all three aspects just described, but, brought together, the composition allows for distinguishing a structure of thinking about empathy against the backdrop of judges in Poland.

References

Batson, C. Daniel. 2009. "These Things Called Empathy: Eight Related but Distinct Phenomena." In *The Social Neuroscience of Empathy*, edited by Jean Decety and William Ickes. 3–15. Cambridge, MA: Cambridge University Press.

Battaly, Heather. 2011. "Is Empathy a Virtue?" In *Empathy: Philosophical and Psychological Perspectives*, edited by Amy Coplan and Peter Goldie. 277–301. Oxford: Oxford University Press.

Camassa, Manuel. 2024. " 'Empathy and Virtue" In *On the Power and Limits of Empathy*. 259–292. London: Palgrave Macmillan.

Carré, Arnaud et al. 2013. "The Basic Empathy Scale in Adults (BES-A): Factor Structure of a Revised Form." *Psychol Assess* 25(3): 679–691. https://doi.org/10.1037/a0032297

Cuff, Benjamin et al. 2016. "Empathy: A Review of the Concept." *Emotion Review* 8(2): 144–153.

Davis, Mark H. 1983. "Measuring Individual Differences in Empathy: Evidence for a Multidimensional Approach." *Journal of Personality and Social Psychology* 44(1): 113–126. https://doi.org/10.1037/0022-3514.44.1.113

Davis, Mark H. 2017. "Empathy, Compassion, and Social Relationships." In *The Oxford Handbook of Compassion Science*, edited by Emma M. Seppälä et al. 299–315. Oxford: Oxford University Press.

Fuller, Melissa et al. 2023. "Empathy Competencies and Behaviors in Professional Communication Interactions: Self Versus Client Assessments." *Business and Professional Communication Quarterly* 86(2): 167–186. https://doi.org/10.1177/23294906221137569

Goetz, Jennifer L. and Emiliana Simon-Thomas. 2017. "The Landscape of Compassion: Definitions and Scientific Approaches." In *The Oxford Handbook of Compassion Science*, edited by Emma M. Seppälä et al. 3–15. Oxford: Oxford University Press.

Guthridge, Michaela and Melita Giummarra. 2021. "The Taxonomy of Empathy: A Meta-Definition and the Nine Dimensions of the Empathic System." *Journal of Humanistic Psychology*: 1–25.

Hall, Judith et al. 2021. "How Do Laypeople Define Empathy?" *The Journal of Social Psychology* 161(1): 5–24. https://doi.org/10.1080/00224545.2020.1796567

Hoffman, Martin L. 2000. *Empathy and Moral Development: Implications for Caring and Justice*. Cambridge: Cambridge University Press.

Jordan, Matthew R. et al. 2016. "Are Empathy and Concern Psychologically Distinct?" *Emotion* 16(8): 1107–1116. https://doi.org/10.1037/emo0000228

Leake, Eric. 2023. *Difficult Empathy and Rhetorical Encounters*. London: Routledge.

Maibom, Heidi Lene. 2017. "Affective Empathy." In *The Routledge Handbook of Philosophy of Empathy*, edited by Heidi Lene Maibom. 22–32. London: Routledge.

Segal, Elizabeth A. 2018. *Social Empathy: The Art of Understanding Others*. New York: Columbia University Press.

Spaulding, Shannon. 2017. "Cognitive Empathy." In *The Routledge Handbook of Philosophy of Empathy*, edited by Heidi Lene Maibom. 13–21. London: Routledge.

Stępień, Mateusz. 2025. "A Developmental Approach to Judicial Empathy." In *Judicial Character in Hard Times: On the Role of Judicial Virtues in Defending the Rule of Law*, edited by Tomasz Widłak. 105–125. London: Edward Elgar.

Tavakol, Sina et al. 2012. "Medical Students' Understanding of Empathy: A Phenomenological Study." *Medical Education* 46(3): 306–316. https://doi.org/10.1111/j.1365-2923.2011.04152.x

von Knorring, Joanna et al. 2019. " 'It is Through Body Language and Looks, But It Is Also a Feeling'—A Qualitative Study on Medical Interns' Experience of Empathy." *BMC Medical Education* 19: 1–8. https://doi.org/10.1186/s12909-019-1770-0

Zaki, Jamil. 2014. "Empathy: A Motivated Account." *Psychological Bulletin* 140(6): 1608–1647.

4 Extracting the role and place of empathy in judicial decision-making

The judge's perspective

Mateusz Stępień

Introduction

Uncontroversial is an assertion that the unique nature of their role has a profound impact on the "empathy labor" of judges. Moreover, their status, tasks, and the context in which they work do not inherently encourage self-reflexivity, particularly concerning the process of empathy labor. This suggests that while it is crucial to explore how Polish judges perceive the actual and prescriptive roles of empathy in their work, it is equally important to continuously highlight the structural features of the judiciary and the place of judges within it. Among others, the structural factors shape thinking and contribute to a partial blindness with regard to empathy labor.

First, operating within a highly structured and normatively defined context, judges engage in a complex set of tasks oriented toward reaching a final decision. Their work often involves repeated, organized interactions with a variety of individuals, mediated by the reading of various documents. Importantly, judges must navigate amidst various subjects (e.g., parties, lawyers, witnesses, experts, other courts, and other judges); they also deal with multiple legal standards and a variety of goals. All of this hinders empathic responses.

Second, judicial decision-making is neither momentary nor loosely structured: Quite the contrary, it is regulated, progresses in stages, and is stretched over time. On the one hand, this provides judges with space for reflection and preparation, destressing as necessary, and strategy-oriented actions. On the other hand, the chances for unstructured and spontaneous displays of easy empathy are minimized. Moreover, if empathic reactions do occur, there is room for neutralizing its consequences, because judges typically anticipate how their behavior, verdicts, and justifications will be assessed by others, especially the parties involved as well as other courts. The need to anticipate reactions makes the use of empathy by judges even more problematic.

Third, judges typically first encounter cases through trial documents, causing subsequent interactions with individuals to be somewhat secondary. Nevertheless, the empathy labor may begin at this initial stage. One judge [32] in our study astutely referred to empathic impulses, describing easy empathy during live interactions in the courtroom. But he noticed a difference when

DOI: 10.4324/9781003546580-5

dealing with written documents, suggesting that impulses are less stimulated under such circumstances: It was easier to maintain an emotional distance. Another judge [6] who works in the commercial division stressed that, in appeals courts, due to the nature of those proceedings, "putting oneself in someone else's shoes" happens during the reading of case files and preparing for hearings. The specificity of appellate litigation undoubtedly transforms a judge's empathic reservoir.

Fourth, judicial decision-making is heavily influenced by a strong professional culture traditionally associated with judicial dispassion (Maroney 2011), symbolized by the metaphor of the "stone" or "poker" face. Expected is that a judge's demeanor signifies impartiality, or at least lends such a perception. Given these factors, it is understandable that caution about utilizing and displaying emotions is readily taken, and, hence, open incorporation of empathy into the decision-making process (or even discussing it) is counterintuitive for justices, even if showing empathy is occasionally what might be needed.

Fifth, despite these challenges, judges are human beings who, as members of society, rely on and utilize empathy in various contexts. The judicial setting does not expunge a judge's general capacity for empathy. Moreover, the judicial system does leave some leeway for judges to manage expressions of (easy or difficult) empathy—hiding or revealing it, with or without substantial or genuine content. In fact, the incorporation of empathy into decision-making processes cannot be eliminated, particularly when this involves relatively uncontroversial aspects such as understanding the perspective of another.

Sixth, different types of legal proceedings, various types of courts, and, to some extent, different objectives call for varying levels of empathy. Due to the diversity within the judiciary, one can initially assume that the scope and role of empathy depend on the court's ranking in the judicial hierarchy, the court's specifications, or even the type of case being handled.

This brief, broad-strokes characterization of some aspects of judicial decision-making underscores deep issues that, on the one hand, encourage limits, caution, and restraint in using empathy and, on the other, show reasons and areas where empathy could be (reasonably more) desirable. This also suggests that structural factors determine the zones within which empathy can be employed.

These remarks are vague and speculative and call for empirical testing. At this point, we problematize the previously described facets of empathy labor in the judiciary, placing the most weight on the perspective of judges. A need for such research has been evidenced not only by a relative, overall silence in the literature of this field but also by a more substantial need for the development of a skillset approach to judiciary reform, including in Poland. In this context, our study raised the following research questions:

- How do judges perceive the actual role of empathy in their work?
- Where do judges see hurdles in legitimate implementation of empathy in the course of their work (stressing the factors that hinder empathy, although it is called for)?

- What do judges think about the normative issue of whether, and for what reasons, judges should or should not be empathetic?

Briefly recapping the methodology underpinning our research study, it should be accentuated that the views of Polish judges were reconstructed through notes from our in-depth interviews (IDIs) and thematic content analysis of the transcripts. The questions posed were carefully designed to align with the various stages of judicial decision-making, aiming to avoid eliciting overly bold or abstract answers. Additionally, we assumed that judges, influenced by a variety of factors, might not typically engage in reflexive consideration of empathy's role within the judicial sphere. The interviews began with general questions about empathy, gradually transitioning to more judicially relevant topics, such as reactions to disputes, the suffering that cases bring, and the idea of showing a human face in the courtroom. Only after these preliminary discussions did we address the most directly pertinent aspects of empathy in the judicial context. After exploring these contextual aspects, we moved on to the normative question of whether judges should or should not be empathetic. This last component often served as the climax of the conversation.

While this interview structure presented certain trade-offs, it was effective in eliciting more than just general, uncontroversial, and safe opinions from the judges. Notably, many judges did commence with preexisting views and familiar conceptual frameworks. However, over the course of the interview, some went beyond their initial positions, opening up to new perspectives and more reflexive stances on the use of empathy. It is clear that the opinions of at least some justices were formed and reformed during the interview itself. The conversational nature (as designed) was crucial to encouraging follow-up questions, examples, and clarifications.

It is also important to note that empathy is a delicate topic, as it places judges in a position where they must critique a concept with generally positive connotations. Additionally, given the political tensions in Poland during the research period, judges might have been hesitant to strongly oppose empathy labor in their decision-making, because such declarations could have created still more negative perceptions of the judiciary among a public that likely lacks a nuanced understanding.

A general outline of judges' views on empathy in their work

Main findings

Considering the aforementioned methodological factors that influence judges' expressions and views on empathy, a key observation is the wide-ranging variations in how judges perceive the role of empathy. Despite their differences, however, it is important to note that all the interviewees in our sample acknowledged empathy's relevance in their work. They diverged only with respect to aspects such as where empathy is manifested, the limits of its scope, and how it fits among other necessary skills. These individual perspectives, though varied, converge on a broader conclusion: a strong positive attitude toward the utility of empathy in judicial functions. When the normative question of whether judges should be empathetic was posed, all judges, without exception, responded affirmatively. However, the degree of emphasis on empathy's importance varied among them. This highlights that while empathy may be approached differently in practice, there is a general consensus regarding its value in fulfilling judicial responsibilities. The findings, which address both the descriptive and normative dimensions of empathy in judicial practice, suggest that empathy is not perceived as controversial by the judges themselves—a perspective contrasting with traditional views. This indicates that, within the judiciary in Poland, empathy is more accepted and integrated into the role of judging than might be assumed.

The transformative potential of judges taking on other trial roles

An intriguing theme warranting closer examination emerged from the judges' elucidations. Some justices mentioned the transformative impact of their personal experiences in other procedural roles, particularly when they took the witness stand during a trial. For these Polish judges, that kind of experience provided insight into how challenging it can be for laypeople to navigate the court system. If even judges, who are well versed in legal procedures, find this experience stressful and unpleasant, how much more difficult must it be for others? Such a shift in perspective has altered the attitude of some judges toward laypeople. As one judge [14] explained, "I had the questionable pleasure of testifying as a witness in court, . . . but it is well known that the position of the accused or a party is more stressful. Simply being there and standing across from someone in a robe, with the chain [of office], is tremendously stressful." Another judge [4] echoed this by recounting how "I was questioned as a witness once in my life and it was also stressful for me." In a sense, this firsthand experience of being a witness, embodying the emotions elicited by this situation (e.g., feeling tense, overwhelmed), altered these judges. Afterward, they were more open to the perspectives of other parties in the courtroom and more sensitive to stressors related to courtroom proceedings. While discussing the cognitive burdens on witnesses during testimony, a judge [33] confessed that despite so many years behind the bench, this was an uncomfortable event. Since then the judge has encouraged judicial candidates to "stand before the court and say something before becoming a judge, because it really opens your eyes."

The realities of the judicial career path in Poland, which adheres to a civil service model, reinforces a limited professional diversity among judges. Since only a small percentage has had prior experience as defense lawyers or public prosecutors, most justices have never worked on or even sat on the other side of the bench. This underlines the importance of diversifying the life experiences of judges and of providing judges with opportunities to directly engage in various legal roles and environments. This diversity could enhance their understanding and empathy, ultimately contributing to a more well-rounded judiciary.

A slip in meaning

It is crucial to note that, in many instances, judges at first defined empathy as distinct from compassion and sometimes as a process not emotionally charged. However, they often later conflated empathy with compassion or with emotional processes. In other words, the unanimous position among judges—emphasizing the distinction between empathy and compassion in nonjudicial contexts—might suggest a similar level of clarity in judicial contexts. Yet despite the clear lines drawn between empathy and compassion, there were many instances during interviews in which the judges explicitly or, more often, implicitly, linked, conflated, or merged empathy with compassion. This slip in meaning is particularly intriguing, as it reveals that judges' perspectives are influenced by shared, underlying beliefs and implied assumptions about correlations between empathy, emotions, and rationality. This, in turn, shapes a kind of cultural script.

One example of this phenomenon involved a judge [22]—well prepared for the interview (as he admitted himself) and aware of the common conflation—who offered a refined definition of empathy that primarily entailed perspective-taking. During our discussion on a proposal to introduce justices of the peace in Poland, the judge shared his direct experiences with term appointment judges, specifically referring to a recent judgment in which two lay judges outvoted a tenured judge, resulting in the acquittal of the accused. Our interviewee emphasized how that verdict was subsequently annulled by a higher court. He characterized the lower court decision as an example of "popular justice," noting that it had little to do with a professional assessment of the evidence, but was driven by "subjective beliefs and empathy [toward the accused]." According to our respondent, the accused in this case was the recipient of empathy from the lay judges who treated him as a "nice guy"; hence, the acquittal was attributed to feelings of pity rather than an objective evaluation of the evidence. Of interest here is that his understanding of empathy presented at the start of our conversation did not align with what the judge articulated later. In the specific case cited, he considered the empathy of the lay judges to be a form of compassion, pity, or sympathy and driven by strong gender-based identification and similarity bias.

Judges' perception of the role of compassion in their work

Main findings

While there has been some scholarly attention on the impact of compassion on judicial decision-making (see e.g., Zipursky 1990; Avgoustinos 2007; Bandes

2017; Del Mar 2017), this subject remains marginalized in academic literature compared to other topics. There is a dearth of research that delves into judges' perspectives and thoughts on this matter: Feeling compassion and expressing it are rarely associated with judging. At the crux of the research informing this book's determinations, our detailed interview guides also investigated what judges face in distinguishing between empathy and compassion. In addition to discussing general linkages between these two, we probed the significance of compassion in the professional milieu of our interviewees. As described earlier, the judges did tend to differentiate between empathy and compassion at the general level, usually adopting a more skeptical view toward the latter. Their frequent associations of compassion with merely emotional responses could lead to a more reserved approach to its use in the legal field. And, in fact, this was the case.

Moving to the main findings, the data indicates that judges are more receptive to the idea of using empathy in legal settings rather than compassion (frequently viewed as disruptive in judicial decision-making). Only a small group (described later) acknowledged that it crops up in the courtroom, while an even smaller group explicitly advocated specifically for judicial compassion. The existence of this last subset is particularly intriguing: Some judges not only admitted feeling compassion but did not see a problem with it. The IDIs we conducted brought to light some of their reasoning on this. Moreover, as will be demonstrated, a few judges described their internal processes in a way suggesting existence of a kind of "compassion labor." By this they meant management or control of their compassionate responses (whose existence they acknowledged) to ensure that their decision-making remains objective and professional.

Second, as already noted, almost all the judges in our cohort clearly distinguished empathy and compassion in the context of their judicial role. Only one judge, a civil court judge [29] with 30 years of experience, presented nuanced responses to each issue that linked empathy to compassion. She admitted that a general understanding of the reasons or impulses for going to court helped her in speaking with individuals in the courtroom and deciding the case: "thus somewhere here this compassion is [located]." Yet she further clarified that "for me there is no equality" between empathy and compassion, although the latter is a part of the former. It was in this interview that the judge explicitly claimed that a judge's compassion is, to some degree, necessary.

Arguments against compassion in the judge's toolkit

The justices in our sample provided several arguments against compassion as an element factored into their decisions. Unsurprisingly, among their different emphases, several interviewees saw compassion's close proximity to emotions as dangerous in the judicial setting. Stronger opposition to compassion labor arose especially among judges working in criminal court divisions.

Serving as a telling example was the opinion of a criminal appellate judge [34] who acknowledged that compassion could lead to an emotional approach to cases and the people involved. While he recognized the importance of being sensitive to others, this justice also believed that compassion entails a significant level of engagement, which could result in a lack of impartiality. In this man's opinion, disengagement is what judges should practice, whereas compassion leads to the opposite.

A similar opinion was raised by another judge [22] who also saw incorporation of compassion within the criminal division as potentially disruptive to a judge's mandated maintenance of (as this judge characterized it) "professional and emotional detachment," underscoring neutrality and objectivity. This connection is telling as it implies that professionalism conflicts with emotionality. At this point the judge provided the example of an actual case over which he presided involving the unfortunate death of a child in a vehicle accident. The judge highlighted the natural inclination to express compassion toward the family of the deceased child. However, a complicating factor was the establishment of the fact that the child was responsible for the accident. This was read by the judge as a warning: "expressing compassion toward the victim or their family would skew my perspective." This spotlighted an overriding principle according to which the judge had to place paramount importance on impartiality, asserting, "I cannot convey compassion in criminal cases, because it is not within my purview. I am not predisposed to express compassion. . . . Certainly, aligning with either party would be deleterious." Another judge [17] who had earlier worked in the criminal division, also referred to potential problems with compassion expressed toward alleged victims. She referred back to her experiences where sometimes the alleged perpetrator has been falsely accused; hence, a compassion reflex would harmfully skew the verdict.

Some judges opposed compassion because it acts destructively; it demands too much from the decision-maker and leads to fatigue. Corroborating this was the opinion of a young assessor working in a civil court division [10] who believed that "there should be less compassion, in order not to additionally burden oneself." It is clear that the justification for eliminating compassion from the decision-making process rested not on the securing of impartiality, but on reducing the emotional burden on the decision-maker. Imposing too much emotionality on judges was seen as detrimental to their well-being. This assessor had some difficulty in grasping empathy and how it correlated with compassion, noting that "it would be hard to do this job if one would like to strongly co-feel with people." In professions dealing with people, compassion should be kept to a minimum to avoid being overwhelmed by the problems of others. Similarly, another judge [17, likewise 21] stated that "if I did not separate [the two], I would not be able to stay at this job and I would not have a private life . . . as it would be too demanding, if I could not separate empathy and compassion in my work." This judge was less concerned about the potential corruption of impartiality and more concerned about the lack of a good work-life balance.

For some, compassion is rather an adversary of judges, but one treated as an obvious fact which requires no explanation. One judge [37] exemplified such a standpoint and, in doing so, undertook great effort to delineate empathy from compassion. For him the former is a matter of adjusting to others, which is uncontroversial and fits the principles of a judicial role, but "not if it would be blended with compassion, which a common bystander feels toward a given person." This man strongly insisted that "I am not directed by compassion in the popular sense of the word." His reasons for this were twofold. First, the judge referred to a normative standard: "I apply statutory law, because this is my responsibility, and I pledge an oath to this." Key here is not to question this as untrue, but to note that this man was reluctant to admit the possibility of being biased by compassion. Second, this justice claimed that he is uninfluenced by compassion precisely because he has become accustomed to human maltreatment, which "for me is not something shocking." That statement expresses not only a strategy of detachment but also exclusion of compassionate reactions. He asked for follow-up queries and wondered about the "neutralization" of compassion: "I suppose that when I came to the court and started judging, I simply immersed myself into some occupational situation, in which I often had to make contact with . . . human harm."

A final argument against judges feeling compassion is particularly intriguing. One of the judges [24] commented that situations arise in judicial work whereby "despite feeling empathy—which involves decoding the feelings of another person, or sometimes even sharing some of these feelings in certain cases—we do not feel, nor should we feel, compassion, because this person does not deserve it." Compassion here was understood as solidarity with a defendant. It is important to note that the judge did not suggest that compassion could compromise impartiality, but rather that it might be morally wrong to feel compassion, for instance, toward the accused. This raises the question of whether such a stance could undermine the presumption of innocence.

Admissions to feeling compassion

Several judges admitted that they have felt compassion while fulfilling their professional obligations, although they strongly differed in their views about its actual and prescribed role. As noted elsewhere, some judges admitted feeling compassion, but stated that this occurred as something of an anomaly or the result of exceptional circumstances; that notwithstanding, the judges claimed that it did not have any significant impact. Along these lines, a civil judge [10], whose skepticism about compassion in the judicial realm was mentioned earlier, described an example later in the discussion. The case involved an alcoholic woman who had been thrown out of her family home and lived in the forest with her partner on retainment; the woman had taken out a high-interest loan and failed to repay it. Despite pitying her situation, the judge concluded that "I can have compassion for this kind of life, let me say it this way, but she has to repay the loan and I awarded the amount that the plaintiff demanded." Importantly, even in this extreme situation, the judge's compassion did not affect the final decision. A similar approach was presented by a civil judge [13], who distinguished compassion from empathy and expressed the opinion that the latter is more adequate for judges. He recalled a case during which compassion broke out pertaining to an elderly woman living alone who was struggling not only with cancer but also huge debt. The issue at hand involved a decision about repossession of her apartment, and, ultimately, it was auctioned off. The judge admitted that "I felt huge compassion toward this lady, huge." This was a sad story, and the internal struggle was difficult, because he felt compassion and wished to help the lady, but the letter of the law was insensitive to the peculiarities of this case. There is a place for compassion, but even in extreme cases it is without impact in legal decisions. Another judge [17], who works in the civil division, noted that in cases involving damages from car accidents, "very often I feel compassion for the situation, but at the same time, I must turn off this compassion." This raises the question of how exactly a deactivation of compassion occurs and what, in that situation, the characteristics of compassion labor are. Similarly, a judge [30] dealing with bankruptcy law, when asked about her experiences with compassion, admitted that "from time to time it happens," but with minor decisions about court costs and when the other party will not suffer a loss. That condition for legitimation of the part compassion can play seems especially intriguing, but the judge did not delve into this further. However, in most cases, acknowledging the presence of compassion went with dismissing its role in the decision-making process, believing that this remains under their control.

The legitimate place of compassion

Judges sometimes admitted to feeling compassion, viewing it as a legitimate reaction rather than an exceptional one, at least to some extent. In certain cases, our interviewees expressed this view, though in relation to specific groups. For instance, a family judge [21] spoke about the impropriety of judges using informal slang to describe parties with psychological disorders, admitting, "I feel pity for [such plaintiffs], simply that." Meanwhile, a judge [11] handling bankruptcy cases in the commercial division reflected on how her emotional responses had evolved over time. Early in her career, she said, "the cases generated tears, identification [with someone], but year by year, some coping mechanisms were developed." This highlighted a gradual process of emotional management. At this point in her career, "I still feel compassion for many people, and I can appreciate my situation . . . however, this is not to say that I am constantly walking around thinking about how unhappy people are." This shows that while there is still room for compassion, it is refined and controlled. Importantly, the judge did not portray herself as devoid of compassion.

Another judge [12] moderated this position by emphasizing "the primacy of facts and professionalism is non-negotiable, and subsequently, when ascertaining guilt, a moment for compassion or considering the need for victim compensation may arise. . . . The ideal scenario entails the victim leaving satisfied; subsequently, the harm incurred should be duly considered." This indicates that while a compassionate stance bears risks and can potentially distort the judicial process, showing compassion after determining guilt—particularly if the reasons for a ruling are explained—can be seen as a manifestation of justice.

A more complex and somewhat incongruous (or perhaps not fully developed) approach to this issue was relayed by a family judge [31] who expressed her thoughts in a rapid, almost fragmented manner. She acknowledged:

> There is compassion, yes . . . the most sorrowful cases are those in which we take children away [from parents], yes. I cannot have compassion for people who drink. . . . But obviously, there are cases when people caring for their elderly parents or sick third parties come [to court], and we allow them to do certain things. . . . They come and say that they need, for example, to repair something. But, on the side, they always talk about how this problem happened, and here is compassion. [Not feeling compassion] we would not be human beings, because everyone feels pity, that these persons have . . . um . . . that their life has worked out in such a way that they have to sacrifice their own life to care for another person. This is when I have compassion, for this person [who is caring for someone].

This judge seemed to view compassion for minors and for people who sacrifice a great deal as caregivers as something normal. However, she clearly established "compassion walls" when it came to parents who have "drunk away [*przepili*] their own children." This selective dispensation of compassion went unquestioned by this justice and seemed to stem partly from the nature of family law procedures, which do not follow the adversarial and oppositional principles typical in other areas of law.

The legitimacy of expressing compassion after a final verdict, particularly during the oral justification and explanation, was highlighted by a criminal judge [1]. He stated, "after passing judgment, when it has already been issued, my possibilities of showing emotions, showing compassion, showing understanding are much higher in the sense that then I can somehow ground why I decided in that way." Notably, this judge grouped emotions, compassion, and understanding into a single category. He further mentioned that "in certain situations, I can even feel compassion toward the accused. But compassion on different levels—let's say, their fate. . . . However, compassion does not necessarily translate into the judgment I will pass." The judge revisited the concept of compassion later when discussing the importance of "showing a human face." He added that he refrains from this in "cases when acting like a human would lead to showing compassion, but this showing of compassion could give the opposing party the impression that I am favorable toward one side." These statements revealed that while the judge recognized the importance of compassion, he was also acutely aware of the potential risks it posed to impartiality. He therefore adopts strategies to manage emotions, allowing him to maintain professionalism while still acknowledging his humanity.

The specificities of family court

Our research was qualitative in nature and not intended to provide a definitive list of factors determining the scope and depth of empathy or compassion experienced and displayed by judges. That remains a challenging issue to investigate in the future. Nevertheless, recognizing that these are, in a sense, only preliminary observations, certain indicators suggest that the type of court division is generally a distinguishing factor. All of the interviewed judges acknowledged the use of empathy in their work, but many specifically spotlighted family courts as those in which the level of empathy is, and should be (in their opinions), greater.

The specificity of family law and the unique demands it places on adjudication emerged as a recurring theme in the judges' reflections. Family judges often emphasized the necessity of empathy in their work, and this sentiment was echoed by judges from other divisions. For instance, a criminal judge [4] remarked that empathy is more crucial in family law, declaring that "a non-empathetic family judge would be a disaster." That reply accentuated a belief that family law cases—often involving deeply personal and emotionally charged issues—require a different, more empathetic approach than other legal domains. Judges identified three main reasons for family law requiring more empathy.

First, judges pointed to the more open-textured nature of family law, allowing more room for employing empathy. This is due to numerous broad-spectrum norms in family law that are open to interpretation (see Kosior, Łukasiewicz 2018). For example, Section 190 of the Family and Guardianship Code (enacted in 1964), concerning limitations of parental custody, requires justices to assess whether the "interest of the child" is at risk. As noted by one judge [21], such assessments often rely on a combination of legal experience and empathy, particularly regarding the child's situation. Some judges expressed even stronger opinions. One family court judge [3] indicated that "the family division is unique; we are not limited by regulations." This demonstrates the exceptionality of adjudication in family cases, which translates into a tendency to apply empathy more broadly.

Second was an observation related to a need to establish long-term relationships with families—something that can only be achieved through empathic acumen. In this vein, one family judge [35] noted that courts with family divisions typically have jurisdiction over specific geographic districts, resulting in long-term engagement with the same families facing structural problems. Such interactions can span years or even decades, fundamentally shaping courtroom dynamics and necessitating more human-centered approaches.

Third, some judges emphasized the necessity of creating a warmer and safer environment in the courtroom, which also requires displays of empathy. In this context, as one judge [3] explained, the key lies in the judge's demeanor—addressing issues in a relatable and humane manner to connect with people. The preferred approach is "a little bit softer, warmer, so that when people come to court, they don't feel like they are speaking to a stone statue. Sometimes, a simple, straightforward manner of speaking is enough to show a human face." This perspective suggests that, in this division, demonstrating empathy through a human face involves moving away from the rigid formalities traditionally associated with the judicial role. The distinctive nature of family cases underscores the importance of fostering a warm and approachable environment. A view expressed by a judge [22] who served 16 years in the criminal courts before transitioning to the family division is particularly telling. He described the experience as moving between "two completely different worlds, governed by different principles." He observed how "switching to the family division is like a complete change in every aspect—the approach toward the parties, attitude toward legal norms, everything is different. Initially, it was a shock. The judge's approach has to be different [in these divisions]." The judge underscored the need for empathy arising from a need to build trust and to establish sturdy relationships with families who are frequently involved in court proceedings. This highlights the multidimensional specificity of family law adjudication.

Mapping the trial stages at which judges declared using empathy

The starting point

Reconstructing where judges' narratives, whether explicitly or implicitly, located the utilization of empathy in judicial decision-making involves distinguishing between two levels. The first focuses on the spheres in which it was declared that empathy operated. This requires attention not only to the areas where judges believe empathy is being used but also to what might be overlooked or left unsaid in their statements. Judges often identified both safer and more controversial areas for employing empathy, particularly when considering the influence of their traditional professional culture. For instance, justices might acknowledge empathy in areas like understanding a legal party's perspective or facilitating communication, while remaining cautious about its use—especially in the courtroom and especially keeping professional restrictions associated with impartiality and detachment in mind.

The second level relates to the functions (or aims) that judges attribute to empathy. Judges identified various roles that empathy plays in judicial decision-making, such as enhancing understanding and communication, ensuring fairness, and (though less commonly) securing their own impartiality. However, it is important to note that most judges did not possess a clear and comprehensive understanding of where empathy fits into their work or what the intended or actual consequences of empathizing might be. As mentioned earlier, there are methodological challenges, because judges are usually disinclined or unprepared to examine the entire decision-making process in its spatial and temporal dimensions, especially when considering established normative standards (desirable functions). Terry A. Maroney and Phillip Ackerman-Lieberman rightly observed that "the debate over empathy can never be divorced from the normative debate over outcomes" (2014: 275). However, in practice, real judges often struggle to establish this link. It is typical for embedded social practitioners, such as judges, to find it difficult to comprehensively problematize their own actions, as their decisions are deeply intertwined with the norms and expectations of their professional culture.

Only by summing up the dispersed thoughts and opinions expressed during interviews can some generalizations be made at the individual level. However, we focused on tendencies and objectives to map the range of judges' thoughts on empathy in their work. This approach looks at overall trends without focusing on specific justices. Taken into consideration is that, for many reasons, it was probably easier for judges to focus on one or more phases of the decision-making process and negatively assess where empathy is not allowed rather than grasp the whole picture.

The judges in our cohort situated empathy within different aspects of their decision-making processes, prompting the question of where empathy is not applied and why. Some judges perceived empathy as a general attitude—a lens through which the entire decision-making process is viewed. Another group of judges considered empathy primarily in the context of managing hearings, focusing on both verbal and nonverbal communication. A third group recognized the role of empathy in establishing the factual basis of the case, such as reconstructing motives, understanding contexts, identifying behavioral triggers, or comprehending the broader circumstances surrounding a case. A smaller group of judges acknowledged the application of empathy in coming to a final decision, as well as to other, less critical determinations made throughout a trial. Additionally, a significant number of interviewees associated empathy with the process of providing justification, particularly during the delivery of oral reasons for a judgment. All these outlooks, except for the first (empathy as a general attitude), aligned with sequential phases in the judicial decision-making process. What follows is a detailed analysis of the judges' perspectives.

Empathy as a general attitude

Describing empathy as a kind of general attitude, several judges saw this response as a broad trait that influences various milieux of judicial decision-making. The justices interviewed saw it as a filter that, among other factors, shapes their judging style, subtly altering how they approach cases and interact with those involved. This perspective suggests that empathy, rather than being confined to specific moments or decisions, permeates their overall approach to the judicial process, affecting how they interpret facts, engage with parties, and ultimately render judgments.

Often empathy was seen as a counterbalance for a mechanization of the judicial process. Along these lines, one judge [11] provided an analogy between dealing with court cases and working in a factory, stating that the dominant principle continues to be that "whatever the consequences are, the law is most important, not persons." In contrast, this judge claimed that, for her, "empathy is important as how I would like to be treated in some office, in such a way I try to treat [both sides]." A critique of the formalism and perfunctory operation of the courts was counterbalanced by this judge's general disposition to apply the Golden Rule—trying to explore how she would like to be approached in court as a party or a witness. Holding such an attitude for a prolonged period would subtly but substantially change the judge's demeanor and actions.

The Golden Rule was brought up in the context of empathy by another judge [21], who emphasized that empathy is a fundamental attitude complemented by specific skills connected with managing the courtroom: "I treat others in the way I wish to be treated myself. This motto I really try to apply." This man converted that mindset into certain judicial behavior: "I always welcome [everyone] kindly, provide basic information about the subject of the hearing, and explain how it will proceed. . . . I express my desire to be seen as someone who will guide the participants through the proceedings. Despite everything, some comfort for the people must be secured, and I am sparked by this in cases." Thus, empathy is considered a more open way of thinking that includes different tangible elements, all aimed at ensuring smooth communication and the well-being of participants by following The Golden Rule.

Another judge [13], who also explored other contexts of using empathy, referred to two general attitudes that shape, according to him, judicial empathy. At first, he spoke about the need to be more tolerant in evaluating others' behavior in the courtroom: "As a young judge, I did not tolerate behaviors such as chewing gum. Today, I do not pay much attention to these details. I am aware that chewing gum helps relieve stress." This requires a deeper understanding of what might trigger participants and what the true aims of the trial are. Next, this interviewee mentioned difficult cases requiring empathy for other reasons. He referred to a case involving the division of an estate after a divorce, during which the ex-wife described a range of abusive behaviors by her ex-husband. The judge wondered, "why didn't the woman mention the physical abuse [earlier, when it happened]?" He reflected on his struggles with understanding the situation and finally acknowledged, "My perspective, [my] rationality is not enough, because I have to be open." Judicial empathy, which is close to tolerance and openness, serves as a tool in avoiding the imposition of a judge's experiences and epistemology on others. Such an attitude, if activated, would subtly transform the entire process of judicial decision-making. The first aspect covers the entire judicial process, while the second one focuses more on establishing the factual basis of a case. Nevertheless, empathy functions as a general disposition.

Several intriguing themes can be identified from the viewpoint shared by a family judge [22] with significant prior experience in the criminal division. His reflections on empathy were characterized by a wider, but integrated approach, offering a holistic view that emphasized connections. Demonstrated was a more comprehensive understanding of empathy that is not very representative of the sample. For him, empathy is a general attitude of not imposing his own standards and experiences on participants in judicial hearings: "I cannot view their lives through the lens of my own life because, at this point, it would be entirely futile." The judge explained that he creates a "thread of sympathy" by reacting in a friendly manner while also understanding the positions and perspectives of the families involved. Only this approach allows him to "try to help them." Central to this is the assumption that these are usually "not normal, working families" and should not be assessed using different "normal" standards. The judge recalled a specific instance where someone refused to have a job and lead a normal life out of fear of a debt collector (***komornik***) coming for debts to be repaid. In response, the judge said, "You, sir, can work illegally, but you should work somewhere." This might be perceived as the judge directing the supplicant to bypass the law, but this was a way of assisting the man, taking his actual circumstances under consideration. In this context, the judge emphasized not imposing his standards on individuals with different life trajectories, reflecting a stance of tolerance or, at the very least, not starting from a position of superiority and unrealistic demands. Here, perspective-taking is the process by which someone's situation is assessed from his or her standpoint without idealization, but with the aim of providing long-term assistance. Empathy involves fathoming the others' circumstances and principles, without imposing unrealistic demands.

The role of empathy in managing hearings

Mentioning the use of empathy in hearings is not a common practice among judges. They may not perceive, or are not accustomed to perceiving, their day-to-day activities in the courtroom in terms of empathy. Instead, judges more frequently refer to the courtroom context and behaviors or reactions that can be interpreted by their discussants as "related to" empathy. This is because, as already pointed out, the concept of empathy itself may not be an obvious point of reference for them. For example, one judge [4] stated: "In our work, one has to be empathetic . . . at least if it is possible." However, upon further probing, it became apparent that this judge, based on her examples and tone, believed that empathy's place is in the courtroom, particularly in the management of hearings. This belief could be inferred from the judge's overall narrative, though not explicitly stated in those terms. Similarly, another judge [26], when asked about the stage in the decision-making process where empathy is relevant, excluded her written opinion but acknowledged its importance "mostly during the process." This pointed to empathy's significance prior to the decision-making, and her examples suggested that it plays a role in managing judicial proceedings. Nevertheless, while some judges directly mentioned the use of empathy for this purpose, a few offered more detailed and carefully considered ideas, rather than just general impressions. Among those who did delve further, empathy was most often related to three specific aspects: a) ensuring the well-being of participants attending the hearings, b) the specific verbal messages conveyed during the process, and c) the strategy of adjusting or accommodating their approach to better suit the needs of those involved.

Ensuring well-being

For some judges, empathy is important because, as one of our interviewees [9] stated, "the people should be taken care of in the courtroom." This includes giving attendees information, so that they "understand what to do and what the consequences are." Such a "taking care of" often involves a specific range of judicial responses that begin as soon as attendees step into the courtroom. In this vein, a judge from a civil division [25], while discussing the relationship between compassion and empathy, stressed the more proactive character of the latter: "I see a human, for instance, who has entered the courtroom. He is lost, does not understand the legal terminology, and I am in a hurry because I have the next hearings. However, I try to explain, to translate, as we used to say, 'from legalese into ours.'" Here, empathy in a judicial context means not being governed by the mechanical, factory-like logic of court proceedings, but rather adapting to the participants in the communicative dimension: recognizing how they might feel in this situation or in a particular procedural role. Such modifications are likely communicated verbally and nonverbally, as well as in judicial behavior. Similarly, another judge [15] mentioned the practice of observing reactions of new individuals entering the courtroom, which can result in the "assessment that they feel lost." These are deliberate actions aimed at ensuring the well-being of the attendees. Another judge [32] directly asserted that "a human face and empathy start from entrance into the courtroom" by the participants; in nine out of ten instances, this constitutes the first time they are in a courtroom. She then reconstructed the typical problems attendees face: how to address the court, where to sit, what the judge expects from them, who is allowed to speak, and so on (see Dudek, Stępień 2021). This judge recounted the message she directs to newcomers, indicating with her hand to "please sit in this place" and speaking "with calm and a smile." If someone openly admitted being in court for the first time, she would add, "The court will explain everything, and everything will be fine." Employment of such simple instruments stemmed from an understanding of the situation that other participants of a hearing were experiencing. Interestingly, as we conversed, the judge asked rhetorically "whether this is empathy or merely professionalism"—raising an issue to be discussed in the conclusion of this chapter.

Another example underlined the importance of an overall planning for judicial proceedings and of having a prior strategy. One judge [4] stated that, based on experience, it is important to allocate more time for each hearing as "life, indeed, surprises." Describing her approach, this judge mentioned, "I aim to reassure [the participants]. By staying calm, I can explain step by step what needs to be done, where they should be positioned, to prevent stress." Ultimately, she devised a protocol to soothe and foster a positive environment in the courtroom. On the one hand, another judge [7] declared that "[a judge] should not succumb to what he feels," but, on the other hand, he also stated that a judge "should always be empathic in the sense of understanding what is happening in the room in terms of peoples' emotions." The accent is placed on monitoring the emotional states of the attendees, which is needed for appropriate judicial reactions.

Over the course of our IDIs, it became evident that judges in Poland repeatedly had trouble providing a clear picture of how they saw the part empathy plays in conducting hearings. Nonetheless, one judge [33], who had read about empathy and had 17 years of experience, explored this topic deeper: "Empathy is important for my work, and I try to cultivate it within myself. This is by gaining a particular skill, but also experience. I know that I am a more empathic person than at the beginning of my career." She spoke about techniques linked to empathy that she had developed herself:

> When people arrive, no matter what I'm dealing with or what might happen later, I always strive to be exceptionally kind. This approach helps to reduce the initial emotions of the arriving individuals. For instance, a divorced couple who may have conflicts with each other—their emotions decrease, leading to a calmer demeanor, which makes the trial easier to manage. Thus, something as simple and common as a smile upon welcoming, and saying a few general words unrelated to the law, really helps. I think this is empathetic and is aimed directly toward the people. This smile can be artificial, forced, or whatever, but that first look, when they are entering the room, when I look at them instead of messing around with the computer or files, when I look at them, smile, introduce myself, and ask them to introduce themselves—really, this works miracles. These people, as I see, talk to me differently.

The judge stated that she was not trained in this direction. When asked why these micro-instruments work such miracles, she responded, "Even a small spark makes a huge effect here because people expect formality and official behavior." Thus, the divergence between what participants anticipate and the courteous judicial conduct they receive generates a distinct attitude among participants. What is intriguing is that this combination of verbal and nonverbal judicial behaviors goes beyond momentary, unplanned connections with someone or an emotional sharing. They are planned, rehearsed, and based on the anticipation of what specific court roles entail. Obviously, the empathic elements are built into specific contexts and harnessed to achieve certain aims, such as the smoothness of the process.

Verbal messaging

Sometimes judges, when speaking of the hearing phase, emphasized the importance of verbal communication as the crux of judicial empathy. For instance, a judge [27] referred to the testimony of an ex-wife's mother in a post-divorce case pertaining to child custody. Observing the woman's very emotional substantiation of the ex-husband's infidelity, the judge (according to her narrative) intervened to say, "The court understands you, ma'am, and believes that this is hard for you. However, these things are important in divorce cases, and the legal provisions say that now this is not important. Therefore, please rest a moment. Do you need to sit down? And then we will come back to the points that are relevant to this case." Here empathy is defined as conveying understanding as well as ensuring that someone's words are heard and taken seriously. The judge also mentioned the practice of asking questions (particularly of witnesses), taking breaks, offering water, opening a window, or permitting momentary rest. Such judicial behavior communicates that she really tries to understand what they are going through.

Likewise, a judge [25] who views empathy on the bench as a form of openness emphasized that "justice is not in the dry paragraphs, but should be directed toward the situation of the other side," thereby highlighting the verbal aspect of his judicial role. He provided an example involving individuals who often fear being judged socially. In one case of eviction involving a drug-addicted daughter, the judge took care to reassure the parents that he was not there to judge their actions. According to his account, people in such situations appreciate when the court shows a human face, demonstrating thoughtfulness rather than handing down moral judgments. The judge remarked that "it is easy to make evaluations until we go through the same thing—suggesting that empathy helps curb the inclination to make snap judgments. The judge further noted that he sometimes relativizes his decision-making power by declaring, "I am not [passing] the Last Judgment. This is not a panel with [persons in robes] who know everything." He believed that such statements do not undermine judicial authority, but rather communicate the practical realities of judicial decision-making. By emphasizing his human face, the judge argues that trust is built among the attendees.

The final example of empathy conveyed through specific verbal communication comes from a family judge [35] who, while reflecting on her overall approach to conducting trials, shared an instance of how she addresses participants: "I understand that you are upset, I realize that this is important, but please don't forget that." The judge associated this with empathy, explaining that such statements are designed to recognize the emotions of the parties involved, while gently steering them toward the legal aspects of the case. This example demonstrates how empathy—or something to which a judge referred by this term—can be seamlessly integrated into judicial communication. All this serves to supervise the emotional dynamics within a courtroom while concurrently maintaining a necessary focus on the judicial process.

Adjusting and accommodating

Among the elements related to management of judicial proceedings, a few judges linked empathy to adjustments and accommodations made—via a judge's behavior, language, and/or demeanor—to the parties or participants (see Dudek, Stępień 2021: 69–73, 172, 186, 202–203; Stępień 2021: 109). Such a strategy satisfies different aims, e.g., protecting the well-being of persons in the courtroom, but also smoothing out the legal process.

One of the judges in our sample [3] justified the need for this kind of accommodation: "We cannot use one overall scheme for everyone, because everyone is different. The level of education and understanding, and how they react, is also completely different. The judge must adjust to the level of those people present in the courtroom." This raised several questions: How is this adjustment applied? How are the levels categorized? And what criteria are used to determine an individual's level?

This could potentially be influenced by a justice's prejudices and/or could minimize the role and range of biases. A judge can employ a set of skills and an open-minded approach to avoid being driven by opening intuitions and premature classification of individuals. According to another interviewee [10], accommodation is necessary because "the court has to lower the language to the level of the witness, as the witness will not reach the level of the judge." Although some might perceive a paternalistic tone, there is a need associated with the establishment of a sense of understanding with the witness—a bond that has cooperative value and does aid in the proceedings.

Similarly, one of the other judges [17] acknowledged that "sometimes this empathy is expressed through different approaches to different people, which I question." For instance, with older individuals who may be intimidated or unsure of courtroom procedures, this judge observed: "They are scared, don't know where to sit, stand, what to say and when, or how to find the room. As a person with social competence, I tend to relax the atmosphere. For me, this is a manifestation of empathy. I recognize their stress and have a measure for addressing it." This judge noted that a common, nonthreatening question—such as asking about someone's age or inquiring about a child's school—can help relieve tension:

> At this moment, laughter occurs and the person begins to relax. I try to empathize with individuals who do not come to court regularly. However, I approach those who are more familiar with the court system differently—there, empathy is not expected. I attempt to apply different behaviors to various types of individuals, but there are limits. For example, if I suspect someone is lying or if the testimony is inconsistent, my empathy ends. This is how it works for me.

One judge [37] presented another facet of empathy in judicial decision-making, characterizing it as a form of "tactful conduct in the broadest sense of the word, depending on the situation, conditions . . . and being patient." This involves "adjusting our communication to the level of the person to which it is directed," complemented by an "ability to navigate the conversation [in the courtroom so] that it aims at establishing a real state of affairs." The judge emphasized that a key aspect of judgeship is investing additional attention in the participants—hence the focus on patience. That additional attention is crucial for uncovering the truth and resolving a case. From this standpoint, empathy in the judicial context is seen as patience and accommodation: "I have to formulate the questions in the language that fits the conceptual apparatus of the person who will be responding to me." This understanding places empathy largely in the realm of judicial proceedings management. When later asked how he recognizes the communication level of the other party and whether this involves complex consideration or comes naturally, the judge described it as an easy task. He elaborated on how the clues inherent in the form and content of the printed motions—such as conceptual apparatus, vocabulary, rules, and syntax—assist in this process. Reflecting on times before the widespread use of computers for preparation of procedural motions and briefs, the judge added a vivid detail: "Often I can imagine someone's living conditions, for example, by the smell of the paper on which a [motion] was prepared—more than once [it was] tobacco smoke, a humbleness, or some mustiness." This example underscores how empathy can involve a keen awareness of context and subtle signals that may guide a judge's understanding and approach to communication during judicial proceedings.

Establishing the basic facts

Some judges envision their empathic approach during hearings as a way to better grasp the factual basis of a case. This reflects a broader perspective in legal scholarship, such as Susan Bandes's (1996: 379) observation that, in criminal cases, "the effort to understand the defendant's perspective can yield information valuable for both the guilt and sentencing phases of the trial." In this context, empathy helps judges with various aspects of arriving at the relevant facts.

For example, one judge [2] declared that empathy is essential in establishing the factual basis for his decision, although it should not affect the judgment itself. This man explained that when trying to ascertain what actually happened, "the broader context and some putting oneself in the situation of these parties, is certainly very useful." This is necessary for examining the details of testimonies and their coherence. This justice further explained that perspective-taking becomes especially key when there are challenges to clarifying the facts: "Quite often, I take the perspective of others to imagine whether the coherence of what a given party is telling us aligns with what I assume they should have done in that situation. Whether both are in line with each other or not—this is very helpful."

Another judge [21] expressed a similar view, arguing strongly for the necessity of empathy in the judiciary and its role in gaining an in-depth understanding of individual behavior. The judge emphasized, "Yes, someone could imagine that these cases should be decided coldly. But this is not correct. Such coldness in proceeding with a case, in fact, does not help in understanding the situation or the feelings of the participants." The judge added that certain elements of a case cannot be fully captured by evidence alone: "Empathy is needed to capture this web of connections related to someone's behaviors. This empathy should be allowed. We should constrain it, but it should still be present. I cannot imagine judges without empathy." This highlights the judge's belief that empathy is crucial for truly understanding the complexities of human behavior in judicial processes. Detached decision-making, in their view, fails to capture the emotional and psychological nuances of cases, making empathy an indispensable tool.

Several judges focused specifically on the role empathy plays in establishing the facts of a case, particularly in relation to testimony. One interviewee [29] placed empathy in the context of discerning the difference between when someone is lying deliberately and when they are struggling to express what they truly mean. Empathy here, according to this judge, encompasses various cognitive processes that help in assessing credibility and intentions more accurately.

In cases involving compensation, empathy also plays a significant role. One judge [13], who had personally suffered a broken leg in an accident, explained how that experience allowed him to better understand the suffering described by victims in similar instances: "When one had a tendon rupture and could not sleep, could not live normally—for me, this is not an abstract thing, and I can understand better the scope of suffering." However, this man seemed unmindful of how his personal experience could actually introduce bias, as he appeared to marginalize the defendant's angle. In this instance, empathy is used in a context that highlights easy empathy, where personal experiences shape a judge's understanding, potentially limiting objectivity.

Another judge [22] extended this argument by referring to the role empathy plays in assessing compensation (*zadośćuczynienie*) for a victim. This justice noted that "being life experienced" helps in understanding the nature of mistreatment or harm, particularly in cases related to marriage and the family. The judge argued that someone lacking a spouse or children might not be able to fully grasp certain situations because they have "idealized images of marriage." The judge also recalled a situation where a supervising social worker, overseeing a child's interests, pointed to a messy room and excessive computer game usage as grounds for the supervision. When asked to elaborate, the judge remarked that a decision-maker without children "looks at this from a completely different perspective" and would lack the practical awareness needed to make a fair judgment. This led the judge to conclude that "judges who have no children should not be working in family divisions—unequivocally."

While these judges emphasized the benefits of empathy in understanding facts and human behavior, they occasionally overlooked the perils of drawing too much from personal experiences. Such a pathway could lead to partial or selective empathy, wherein a judge's private experiences may distort his or her objectivity. Nonetheless, the examples extracted from our interviews illustrate that empathy is viewed as an important tool by many judges, whether in interpreting testimonies or making connections with the parties involved. Concurrently, these judges' reflections reveal a delicate balance between using empathy to understand the emotional complexities of a case and maintain impartiality and avoid bias.

Decision-making

Judges are typically highly skeptical about using empathy during the closing phase in which they reach a final decision. For example, a judge [8] who emphasized the importance of empathy also argued that decision-makers should "have this empathy well balanced . . . not [go to] any excesses, and thus, not be empathic too much, because it disturbs the judging. . . . Too much empathy can paralyze the decision-making." From his viewpoint, disproportionate empathy can undermine objectivity. However, utilizing empathy in other phases of the trial—such as during examination of the testimonies or understanding the context of the case—is more widely accepted. These phases offer a safer harbor, allowing judges to remain impartial while using empathy as a tool to aid understanding.

Despite an overall hesitancy to employ empathy in the final verdict, a few interviews suggest that some judges did see a limited role for it in this process. For example, one judge [11] placed empathy within the decision-making phase, noting the importance of "put[ting] myself in [a party's] position. Maybe not during the hearing and direct contact, but during the evaluation, to understand what she thought—the understanding should be primary." This suggests that empathy is useful for a broader comprehension of the parties' perspectives after the hearing phase.

A criminal judge [4] explicitly stressed that empathy plays no role in determining guilt or whether prohibited acts occurred. In Polish criminal law, where the final sentencing includes both the determination of guilt and the imposition of penalties, empathy does not affect the former. However, empathy becomes relevant when choosing penal measures, as it helps in adjusting these to fit the social circumstances of the convicted individual. This aligns with research on the role of empathy in sentencing (e.g. Chin 2012; Cormack 2021). Another criminal court judge [14] similarly emphasized the need for empathy, particularly during sentencing, stating that it helps in "track[ing] their motivations." Here, empathy allows the judge to understand the broader circumstances and life conditions of the convicted, leading to a more human-centered approach to sentencing. This attitude shifts away from strict formalism and toward a more context-sensitive form of judgment. This point was also explored by another judge [36], who argued that empathy means "not sticking to icy procedures in situations where there is a choice to use a less icy procedure or base [the decision] on a different interpretation."

A family division judge [3] provided an original perspective, arguing that empathy directly influences how she interprets the law. She explained that empathy allows her to focus more on the goals of her judgments and on the individuals whose problems she is resolving. This judge observed that younger justices tend to focus on "ideal interpretations" of the law, without considering the human problems before them, whereas a more experienced, empathic judge considers the consequences of a decision for the individuals involved. According to this judge, empathy can shift a decision from a literal application of the law to a more consequentialist approach, where the impact on people is a primary concern. This perspective stands out, as it suggests that empathy is integral to judicial decision-making—not just as a tool for understanding, but as a guide for interpreting the law itself.

Another family judge [21] also emphasized the necessity of empathy, particularly in countering prejudices. He stated that "entering their situation shakes off some manner of prejudice. . . . Empathy is, in fact, such a counterbalance to these prejudices, especially when we are deciding cases." This judge explicitly saw empathy as crucial during the decision-making phase, helping to challenge biases and ensure fairer judgments.

Overall, whereas many judges are cautious about allowing empathy to influence their final decisions, others recognize its value in humanizing judicial processes. In sentencing, family law, and understanding motives, empathy helps judges move beyond formal, legal interpretations to address the human side of each case. However, this approach remains controversial, as many judges continue to emphasize the need for balance to avoid undermining impartiality.

Justifying

In examining another phase of the trial where judges declared using or showing empathy, comprehension of the structure of court procedures in Poland is key. Polish procedural law distinguishes between presenting the oral motives for a verdict during the concluding hearing of a trial, on the one hand, and providing written reasons in a judicial opinion, on the other hand. The written opinion is produced either upon a party's request or when the judge is legally obligated to provide it. In minor criminal cases, these written opinions are structured using a pre-established form, making it harder for judges to include less formal, more authentic narratives. In civil cases, transcribed oral motives can sometimes be formalized into written opinions, but this is rare. Typically, oral and written justifications are distinct in terms of style, length, and tone.

Interestingly, although judicial opinions vary, most judges recognize the significant role of empathy in justifying their judgments. This finding, while unexpected, shows that empathy plays a role beyond simply knowing the facts. However, this should not be taken as evidence that all judges have a well-developed perspective on or experience in this matter. Some judges made only brief remarks on this aspect. For instance, one judge [19] mentioned, "Yes, empathy is applied, but only during the justification phase." Another justice [12], upon reflection during the interview, remarked, "Maybe this could be a tool in the justification phase. I hadn't thought about this before and need to reconsider."

Some judges provided a broader understanding of empathy's role. Several indicated that, after the verdict is announced, there is more room for expressing empathy. The post-verdict phase allows for a reduction in the formality of the proceedings, permitting more personal remarks. One of our interviewees [6] explained that "The issue is the extent and timing of externalizing empathy" and noted that "a perfect moment for showing empathy is during the provision of reasons (*uzasadnienie*)." This phase offers judges a safer space to demonstrate empathy without risking neutrality.

This suggests that while empathy may be utilized during the trial, its overt expression is often considered more appropriate only after the verdict is delivered. Some judges even raised the possibility of displaying empathic language without genuinely experiencing empathy, suggesting a strategic use of the empathy instrument to maintain judicial decorum while still engaging the parties.

Judges more frequently discussed empathy in the context of the oral remarks than in the written opinions. Orally delivered motivations allow for a more informal, expressive mode of communication, while written opinions are typically highly formal, serving as the basis for any potential appeals. Nevertheless, one judge [24] admitted to incorporating empathy into his written opinions, though his description of this practice was cursory. The flexibility permitted during the oral remarks allows for the expression of understanding and emotions—elements that are harder to incorporate into the rigid structure of written opinions. Another judge [17] described those closing remarks as an ideal opportunity to convey a deeper understanding of the parties' situations and even to express emotions. A judge [6] who advocated for careful use of empathy suggested that manifesting an understanding of a party's situation helps them feel acknowledged: "I understand and considered the motivation of the party [in the legal proceeding] . . . in order to make the party feel like a subject." Similarly, another judge [30] emphasized the importance of ensuring that "People feel that I understood them, that their arguments were reflected upon. . . . They may not remember how the judge looked or his or her name, but they will remember whether they were understood and whether their claims were acknowledged, even in general terms." Another judge [3] echoed this sentiment, underlining that it is essential for parties to feel that "the court tries to understand their positions. . . . It is not the case that the court is solely driven by legal norms and lacks any feelings." This allows the court to communicate empathy without undermining legal authority.

That said, certain judges distinguished between empathy in oral and written opinions. One judge [20], for example, did not see empathy's role in written opinions but emphasized its importance in creating the impression that "they were listened to, their arguments were taken into account, evaluated, and commented on." He explained, "I try, through my questions, behavior, and way of proceeding, to create a situation where the party does not leave the court with the belief that I made a decision while completely ignoring their arguments." This use of empathy enhances the perception of fairness and consideration, particularly during the justification phase.

This approach aligns with procedural justice principles, which emphasize the importance of parties feeling heard and respected during legal proceedings. As Tom Tyler noted, "When authorities are presenting their decisions to the people influenced by them, they need to make clear that they have listened to and considered the arguments made" (2000: 122). Judges' efforts to convey empathy reflect a broader judicial aim to ensure that parties perceive their treatment as fair, though this may be more strategic than genuinely empathetic.

Some judges articulated that ensuring parties that feel heard is especially crucial when communicating unfavorable decisions. For example, one judge [16] noted that if parties feel listened to, they are less likely to perceive the decision as arbitrary and are more likely to accept it. Another judge [18] described empathy as a way to convey that, while the court understands the person's situation, courts of law are constrained by legal boundaries. This approach aims to foster understanding, even if it does not involve genuine empathy. A judge [3] described usage of a rhetorical style in cases where the court acknowledges a party's efforts but finds them insufficient. This is more of a strategic communication tool than an expression of deep empathy. Another judge [5] mentioned the importance of communicating final decisions in such a fashion as to demonstrate that all claims were considered; this helps to soften the blow of an unfavorable ruling. Similarly, a judge [29] explicitly discussed using phrases like "I understand your situation" as she read her oral motives to frame her legal decisions within the boundaries of empathy, explaining the reasoning behind the judgment while offering understanding to the parties. This approach is intended to mitigate the negative impact of losing while reinforcing the fairness of the process.

Overall, judges identified several purposes served by empathy in this field: a) achieving procedural justice, b) softening the impact of bad news, c) enhancing the judge's comfort, d) fostering empathy toward the judge, and e) reducing the scope of appeals. Despite these varying motives, the core message remains consistent: The court aims to show that it understands and considers the positions of both sides. This communication is often framed in empathetic language, but whether it reflects genuine empathy or strategic behavior remains a subject of debate.

To manifest or not to manifest empathy: that is the question

Initial thoughts

The preceding discussions aimed to map how judges position empathy within various stages of judicial decision-making. However, another crucial aspect to consider is whether judges choose to demonstrate empathy and how they justify these choices. This issue has been touched upon earlier—for example, effective use of empathy during hearings often requires its explicit demonstration or, at the very least, an expression of empathetic understanding. However, some in our cohort of judges argued against displaying empathy. The decision to manifest or suppress empathy is significant because it offers valuable knowledge about how judges engage in empathy labor. Understanding the pressures on judges to regulate their empathetic expressions deepens our comprehension of that labor, which entails, among other things, a sustained effort to control emotional responses to meet the expectations of impartiality and detachment that are fundamental to their role.

This concept can be better understood by referring to the work of Arlie Hochschild, a pioneer in the field of emotion regulation. Hochschild described two strategies that workers use to conform to "feeling rules," which are socially shared guidelines about when and how to engage in certain emotions and whether and how to manifest them externally (1983; with reference to the judicial context, see also Bladini, Blix 2022: 240). The first strategy—"surface acting"—involves displaying emotions that do not match one's actual feelings such as workers feigning emotions that comply with prescribed feelings or display rules. The second strategy—"deep acting"—involves modifying one's inner emotions to genuinely align with the expected display rules.

This framework can be extended to empathy regulation among judges to match the display rules of their social role and professional culture. Judges may pretend to be detached (engaging in surface acting) even when they internally feel empathy, or they may strive to genuinely detach themselves (deep acting), thus adjusting their behavior to expected norms. Additionally, judges may engage in verbal and nonverbal communication that mimics empathy but serves more as a rhetorical gesture than a reflection of genuine empathetic thought.

It is important to recognize that both difficult and easy empathy can be activated internally without being outwardly expressed. The former involves sustained, deeply ingrained cognitive processes, making the question of whether to manifest it more complex. This contrasts with the latter, which is often more transient and situation specific. Manifestations of these two types differ meaningfully due to these intrinsic characteristics.

Interestingly, a few judges [6, 24] called attention to evolving norms regarding expressions of empathy, noting a shift from traditional judicial training that discouraged shows of emotion toward a more moderate approach that allows room for some empathic display. On the one hand, this indicates a growing openness to expression of certain emotional states, including empathy. On the other hand, this does not imply a complete abandonment of the rigid stone-faced demeanor typically associated with judges, but rather involves discerning when and which emotional responses are permissible and what objectives they serve. According to a judge [6] with decades of experience in various divisions, "the problem still lies in the thin boundary between what is permissible in showing empathy, emotions, and sensations, and what constitutes a transgression of these boundaries." Despite the existing problem, he argued further that this does not mean judges should play it safe, consistently adhering to a detached demeanor.

Despite these observations of changing instruction and practices, directly asking judges whether they manifest empathy is challenging. The very question meets established judicial standards, values, and principles head on; judges may be hesitant to question these openly. Moreover, as seen, perceptions and definitions of empathy naturally vary—especially considering its emotional aspects and especially considering the judicial context. There is also the problem of whether empathy constitutes an emotional response or a cognitive process or both. Some theoretical approaches highlight the empathizer's response, often verbal, as a core component of empathy, setting "rhetorical empathy" apart as a form of communication aimed at achieving empathic goals. All of this notwithstanding, we were able to draw informative findings from our research into the views of Polish judges with regard to manifesting or suppressing empathy.

Experiencing but not manifesting empathy

Many judges acknowledged, directly or indirectly, that they do experience empathy at certain stages of a court case (particularly during hearings) but often consciously stifle its external manifestation. For instance, one judge [6, likewise 3] referred to instances where he felt empathy without showing it. Nevertheless, he conceded that "Contrary to appearances, empathizing by judges happens very often." This self-restraint in expressing empathy, as the judge explained, stems from the traditional training of judges in Poland, which emphasizes avoidance of anything that could be taken as a sign of partiality: "The demand for full impartiality necessitates minimizing the display of emotions. The pursuit of complete impartiality has led to the belief that showing empathy or compassion in the courtroom is improper. This is how we [judges] have been nurtured and trained." Again, that training has inculcated internal processes of monitoring, controlling, and redirecting empathic impulses.

Another judge [19], when asked about feeling but not showing empathy admitted: "It happens. I see someone describe their living situation, and I think—I had such a situation once. I understand this and try not to show it because I must remain impartial. Then I say to myself, 'stone face, stone face, yes.' This is our job to somehow ensure this impartiality." This judge clearly referred to external impartiality but overlooked how experiencing empathy internally might still affect him. Notably, the stone-face concept functioned as a self-management tool, helping this judge in his surface acting.

Some judges' disclosed stronger internal struggles. One judge [4], reflecting on her long courtroom experience, remarked:

> I can have my feelings. I can understand a person, or at least I try to. However, my role in this room means that I cannot show this. I cannot say, 'I have compassion for you, ma'am,' because this would suggest that I believe her, that I find her credible. Therefore, even though I have thoughts and feelings like any human, I often cannot express them in the courtroom.

This statement implies a tension, with the judge viewing the inability to express empathy as unfortunate. Additionally, the judge suggested that avoiding empathy is necessary to prevent communication failures compromising the outward show of impartiality. However, this raises the question of whether any and all displays of empathy pose a risk. Examples of directly expressed compassion highlight the nuanced boundaries judges navigate.

Another telling perspective was expressed by a judge [15] who noted that "An empathic judge can be impartial, but if he shows empathy too much, the other side might think the judge is biased. Therefore, we cannot show empathy or emotions and must maintain a stone face." Characteristic is the stone face seen as both empathy's antithesis and a strategy to ensure that hidden empathy does not tear the veil of impartiality (see Bergman Blix, Wettergren 2018). In this case, too, a judge assumed that surface acting suffices to prevent accusations of bias; the problem again lies not in the empathic impulse itself, but in its expression. This stance focuses solely on external perceptions and does not consider whether internal empathy might also affect decision-making. Interestingly, the judge's statement that empathy should not be shown "too much" suggests that, in fact, a degree of externalization is permissible.

Some judges provided a closer look at a more wide-ranging rationale for not manifesting empathy. A criminal judge [24], trained in the "old school" approach to court proceedings, described the overall tendency within the judiciary:

> Judges experience emotions, perhaps not all of them, but those empathic ones, even if they don't display them openly. For example, I tend to show my emotions, albeit not always. Some colleagues almost never show empathy in the courtroom. Still, outside the formal setting, I sense their feelings—they share them with me or the secretary outside the courtroom. They wear a kind of mask in front of the parties involved. They feel, but it is not always apparent. This is why people perceive judges as nonempathic, because they usually don't display empathy openly. Most judges believe, rightly, that they should refrain from showing these feelings until the verdict is delivered. Some choose not to display empathy

> even after the verdict. The robe and chains [of office] create an immediate emotional distance, reinforcing the impression that judges lack empathy.

This judge emphasized that while judges do experience emotions, including empathy, they are expected to limit these expressions in court. This suggests a conscious regulation of outward behavior, influenced by the symbolic elements of judicial decorum, which can create a perceived emotional distance. The judge's reflection on these symbols—such as the robe and chains of office—as contributing to perceptions of judges' emotional detachment highlights how courtroom decorum shapes both behavior and expectations, influencing the perceived role of empathy in judicial practice.

Several judges expressed strong opposition to displaying empathy, often justifying this stance with reference to impartiality, although they admitted to experiencing empathy under extreme circumstances. For instance, a family judge [21] discussed the internal work of not showing empathy, commenting:

> Controlling empathy should be my main task. I often deal with harm related to the child of a spouse. If I were to show empathy to one side, it would lead to accusations of partiality. Empathy is in the back of my mind—do not confuse this with sympathy. Empathy will certainly impact my decision, but I must monitor myself and not show it. However, when I meet the child alone, I can allow myself more openness.

This self-monitoring process points to a learned effort to act contrary to natural, empathic impulses, which would normally be expressed instinctively.

Another judge [18] admitted that he empathizes, but only in specific cases, such as when individuals have suffered greatly and are not morally responsible for their actions, like failing to pay bills: "I understand the situation, but rarely do I allow myself to show this understanding emotionally." That segregation suggests that empathy can closely resemble pity or frustration. It also hints at a differentiation between expressing empathy emotionally and safely, but non-emotionally, as noted by another judge [12]: "Sometimes it happens that I do not show empathy, and sometimes I manifest it sparingly."

Admitting to expressing empathy

Only a few judges admitted to actually expressing empathy, either occasionally or as a regular practice. Among those who did, a commercial judge [9] handling private bankruptcy cases stated he has no issue with expressing empathy. However, this approach reflects the specific nature of proceedings in that division, typically involving only one party. The absence of opposing sides alleviates concerns about partiality, allowing for a more empathetic approach.

Conversely, some judges allow the expression of empathy primarily as a stress-relieving tool. For instance, a judge [11] stated that whereas he generally refrains from showing empathy in the courtroom, he occasionally does so to minimize participant stress. He described his approach as "just stroking [someone's] head" or saying, "I understand that you are in a tough situation." However, he stressed the importance of restraint, emphasizing that "the court should not give the impression of being more favorable to one party over the other." Similarly, another judge [2], who defined empathy as perspective-taking, stated that he tries not to display empathy toward anyone: "It seems to me that professionalism involves not showing any emotions or personal feelings about what is happening." He makes exceptions when witnesses experience extreme distress, allowing himself to "show more kindness." He emphasized that his approach to empathy is distinct from emotionality, aiming to avoid displays of his own emotional state in court.

The well-being of participants was also a concern for another judge [23], who—when asked about suppressing an experience of empathy—shared a story about the eviction of an elderly woman with health issues: "I tried to make her feel comfortable in the courtroom, to ensure that she felt good here at least. I even sat next to her, helped her speak, and when she started to whisper, I approached her as a human . . . to make the process as painless as possible." This justice emphasized the lasting impact of this encounter: "I remember this to this day. It was a significant experience." While the judge's actions may have reflected compassion rather than empathy, her deep consideration of the woman's perspective was evident.

One judge [29] argued that showing certain types of empathy in the courtroom can be necessary: "If I give people the impression that I understand them—even if I do not fully understand, I will be frank with you—this causes them to open up and talk more to me." For him, demonstrating understanding, which must be felt and seen by others, serves an instrumental purpose, influencing the behavior of individuals in the courtroom.

Some judges adopted a situational approach to this matter. A criminal judge [1] explained, "In some situations, judges can show empathy, but, in others, absolutely not. If we talk about what is inside me, that is inside [me], then for sure they [judges] should [be empathetic]. The question is how [they] can show [empathy] in certain situations." He emphasized the importance of avoiding actions or words that could cast doubt on the court's objectivity. Yet another judge [20] elaborated on situational empathy but was careful to differentiate it from compassion: "I try to show empathy always if there is such a will on the other side, and there are no barriers, limits, or hostility directed toward me. There is definitely no place for showing compassion. . . . Empathic behaviors are not instances of showing impartiality: they result from a willingness to calm the situation down and are based on legal rules and principles of politeness." For him, the attitudes of the active parties are key in deciding whether to express empathy, and these actions serve a soothing function with clearly defined limits.

Only a single criminal court judge [14] viewed manifestations of empathy as normal courtroom practice:

> I always try to show respect and openness toward the people I meet in the courtroom. Some think I am exaggerating and that criminals should not be treated this way. . . . There are attempts to exploit this [approach], but I set limits for myself. I try to be open, understand others, and listen to what they say between the lines. This is beneficial for them, but I feel it is mostly beneficial for me; I feel that I am doing my job well.

This judge's approach reveals how empathy can sometimes border on emotionality, emphasizing mutual benefits and personal fulfillment in the judicial role.

Summing up, judges often feel empathy in court but hide it. Their training, judicial standards, and worries about how they are perceived lead them to suppress outward signs of empathy. Maintaining a stone face, doing surface acting, means control over their emotions and public image. This self-regulation comes from a judicial culture valuing emotional restraint to protect impartiality while navigating courtroom complexities. However, judges rarely reflect on how empathy might affect their decisions. They focus on preventing any perception of bias through outward displays. A few judges suggest carefully calibrated expressions of empathy might not always compromise impartiality (see Chapter 5). This hints that the role of empathy in judicial practice may be more nuanced and intricate than traditionally understood.

Obstacles in employing empathy

Barriers vis-à-vis limitations

Most judges in the research sample recognized the importance and value of empathy in certain circumstances or in specific phases of decision-making. Nonetheless, in the majority of instances, even after recognizing the significance of empathy, the interviewees in our sample underscored the constraints and potential hazards of its application in the judicial domain—the limitation of empathy was a common motif. Yet here it is important to differentiate limitations from actual barriers precluding the use of empathy in situations where many would consider it necessary and appropriate. Over the course of our interviews, judges highlighted three main clusters of obstacles: a) the attitudes and mindsets of judges themselves, b) the organization of their work, and c) an inclusive category with less prominent factors. Therefore, these factors under consideration limit the scope of empathy's positive impact on decision-making process, as perceived by judges.

The "chain of office syndrome"

Delving into the first of these obstacles, often discussed by the interviewees was a specific attitude and mindset, found among many judges and known in professional circles as the "chain of office syndrome." This term refers to the heavy chain necklace that Polish judges wear as a symbol of their power. The expression—since it dubs some practices as an illness or disorder—already implies a negative assessment of such a mentality. Importantly here, the chain of office syndrome was mentioned by a few of the judges in our sample as a factor that limits the ability to empathize. Various versions of this syndrome surfaced in our conversations (for descriptions of related phenomena, see, e.g., Posner 2013: 146–156). Describing the phenomenon, one judge [2] explained:

> The chain [of office] illness is the syndrome of a judge who is somewhat burnt out professionally, around 50 years old, and who perceives himself as almost godlike. Cases bore him, because he believes he already knows in advance what each party is going to say. He is overconfident about the verdict. Thus, all the required work becomes unnecessary, a waste of time and effort, leading to arrogant behavior.

Such judges have lost the humility needed to remain approachable and attentive, gradually becoming more closed off. According to the characterization noted earlier, it is experienced judges who are more likely to be affected by this syndrome, which leads them to assume they are always correct because of their extensive experience on the bench. This results in a lack of curiosity and open-mindedness. Judges suffering from chain of office syndrome believe that their judgments (or views) are superior, leading them to disregard the worth of other people's emotions and opinions.

Another judge [26] offered a wholly different observation, seeing this disorder as primarily affecting younger judges. She reflected on her own unpreparedness when she began her career as a 20-something judicial officer. She pointed out a shared mentality among young judges, describing it as an overconfidence symptomatic of chain of office syndrome: "After the exams and nomination—for sure I know better, and I don't have any doubts." She admitted that she, too, had been touched by this syndrome at the beginning of her career, when there is a tendency to quickly handle cases, trust one's own knowledge, and be convinced of one's own infallibility. This woman believed that her professional development has been linked to increasing empathy rather than following what chain of office syndrome dictates. She asserts that "The older I am, the more sensitive I become."

Our cohort of judges also articulated broader perspectives on the obstacles preventing judges from utilizing empathy effectively. One judge [6] mentioned a lack of time, a high level of routinization, and specific attitudes found among judges. He asserted that "there is no point in denying that simply being a judge means having significant power at your disposal, which operates uniquely. And something, which I call (with a smile) 'an occupational disease,' meaning the overall recognition that one is always right, resulting in being less inclined to empathy, to understand, and to engage in any discussion." In this case, the use of empathy was seen as the opposite of always having the correct answer.

Some individuals among our sample described a similar phenomenon but did not apply the same term. One judge [30] noted instances of inappropriate conduct by justices: "I sometimes get the feeling that judges, after years of judging and a particular upbringing, exhibit a behavior that can be described as exalting in power, and this applies also to judicial power." That description aligns closely with a pretentiousness that is characteristic of chain of office syndrome. A lack of readiness to dialogue was highlighted by another judge [9], who stated that "A judge cannot get accustomed to their own conceptions, to what he was prepared for. My colleagues [private legal representatives] tell me that they know exactly when a judge has already entered [the courtroom] with a conception in his head of how to solve the problem. And during testimony, when a fact occurs that points in the opposite direction, he'll become impatient and irritated." These symptoms are also related to the chain of office syndrome; the emotional annoyance of such a judge stands in stark contrast to the calm, sensitive, and empathic approach. A similar concern was raised by a civil court judge [29], who emphasized the inverse of empathy, such as being overly meticulous and applying radical formalism. According to her, an attitude sometimes manifested communicates to others that "There's no point in getting into someone's feelings and thoughts, because I know what's going on perfectly." Such a stance hinders both individualization and a focus on resolving problems.

Summing up, the chain of office syndrome concept highlights a critical challenge within the judiciary: the potential erosion of what empathy and openness does exist due to entrenched attitudes and posturing. As illustrated by our cohort of judges, this phenomenon can manifest itself at various stages of a judge's career, impacting both seasoned and novice judges, albeit differently. Experienced judges may become overly confident and dismissive, while younger ones might exhibit a premature sense of infallibility. Both scenarios underscore the importance of fostering empathy and humility within the judiciary to ensure fair and sensitive handling of cases. Addressing these issues requires a concerted effort to promote continuous self-reflection, professional training, and an emphasis on the human aspects of legal proceedings. Ultimately, cultivating a judiciary that values empathy and open-mindedness will lead to more just and effective outcomes for all involved. To put it simply, developing empathy is a way to treat and perhaps cure judges of chain of office syndrome.

Structural and organizational factors

Another set of elements that contributes to difficulties in employing empathy includes structural and organizational barriers. Among other things, a managerial style of work organization—with a particular emphasis on statistics such as case closure rates, trial duration, and the success of appeals in higher courts—was identified by judges as a barrier.

For example, one judge [34] conveyed this by stating that, "Statistics can kill sensitivity. . . . There is a difference between the judiciary and the bakery." There is a vast difference in the output and the process of delivery in the two spheres: Dissimilar is management, the product's tangibility, and the delivery method. Thus, the criteria for evaluating judicial work cannot be analogous to work in a bakery. In a similar vein, another judge [2] stated: "We just want to end the case and move on to another one . . ., and, in fact, we are not accountable for being empathetic, but for how many cases we finish and in what period of time." Yet another justice [8] highlighted the task-oriented nature of the profession, limiting space for empathy.

A common hindrance to empathy utilization is the pressure of time constraints and overwhelming caseloads (as described, among others, by judges 7 and 8). These matters point to a wide spectrum of organizational and systemic factors. A judge [37] who characterized empathy in the judicial context as "patience and accommodation" emphasized insufficient time to patiently "[render a decision] with recognition of the just interest of the parties." There remains potential for the decision-maker to combine such patience and accommodation only by working additional hours. This judge admitted, "I'm working every Sunday." The shortage of time, coupled with case overload leading to overwork, "generates, even in cases of judges with an angelic character, certain emotions that are far from empathy." In other words, under such structural conditions, emotional reactions tend to lean toward the opposite of empathy. Another justice [4] also delved into the repercussions of the "pressing of time" manifesting in real-life situations: "There is no time for, I know, to say one or two sentences to this person, in order, for example, to calm him down, as we see that he is nervous." This is due to people waiting in the courthouse hallways for the next hearing. As the judge summarized, "There is not enough time to be empathic in the courtroom."

Conversely, empathy is portrayed here, in the court context, as an appropriate reaction to stress and a means of providing necessary measures. The "extent of the work" was brought up by a different judge [2]. Under such circumstances, "it's hard to invest enough time, attention and focus . . . some kind of turning off happens. . . . Thus, the amount of work is hugely important." Worth noting is that turning off easily leads to insensitivity. A different judge [10] declared that "we should be careful with empathy, because cases have to be resolved in order to deal with [the next] one." Of course, one could ask if caring about the cases at hand as well as those pending is already a kind of empathy. Still another justice [18] stressed the huge overload of cases: He mentioned a family judge he knows who prepares ten opinions a year, while he, in a different division, deals with ten in a week. Researching the deeper background, preparing more thoroughly for the next hearings, and writing well-prepared judicial opinions are time-consuming tasks. What is missing, as the judge pinpointed, "is the parties feeling that their voices were heard and given attention." Harking back to the bakery analogy, another judge [17] commented on the "lack of time and case overload . . . [as] if we're working in a screw factory of cases . . . lack of time and rushing." According to one judge [6], the vast burden of work might create a situation in which a judge could react with "standoffishness and a kind of artificial 'infliction,'" leading to "negative feelings which are incompatible with sensitivity."

Recapitulating, conversations with judges about empathy and law in the context of the Polish judiciary revealed significant structural and organizational challenges impeding effective use of empathy in judicial proceedings. An emphasis on managerial efficiency, whereby statistics and case throughput take precedence, creates an environment that stifles sensitivity and individualized attention. Judges highlight the incompatibility of treating judicial work like a factory operation, which diminishes the space for empathy. Overwhelming caseloads and time pressures exacerbate the problem, leaving little room for judges to engage empathetically with legal parties in the courtroom. The need for systemic change that prioritizes the quality of judicial engagement over mere statistical accomplishments becomes evident. Adjusting case management practices and providing judges with the necessary resources and support to manage their workloads effectively are crucial steps toward fostering empathy within the judiciary in 21st-century Poland.

Other factors

The judges we interviewed pointed out several miscellaneous but noteworthy obstacles which are therefore presented separately here. For instance, one judge [10] identified the problem of "evolving procedural law that limits the judge's discretion." A consequence of this is that a justice's discretionary power has been greatly reduced, and the remaining margin of freedom leaves little room for employing empathy. Other issues that arose include "the lack of a cooperative attitude on the part of participants in proceedings," which some of our interviewees even interpreted as "a form of aggression" [12]. Even microaggressions can affect a judge's proclivity for empathy, transforming emotional responses into defensiveness. Similarly, another judge [34] sees "a lot of unneeded antagonisms," which are sometimes made manifest as accusations against the judge: "You are biased."

Moreover, according to one judge [19], a burnout syndrome also afflicts legal professionals, particularly people who "feel above average," but also those with "a higher personal sensitivity"; this can lead to capitulation and a switching off of empathy as a psychological defense mechanism. Reflecting on this problem from his own experience, this man divulged that, "I burned myself out twice. . . . And the thing I am most afraid of is burnout for the third time. And I was exhausted exactly because of empathizing." Thus, empathy under such circumstances can incur costs, leading to personal crises and suffering. Another judge [24] admitted that he does not have time for empathy. Reflecting on the shortcomings of empathy in a uniquely constrained milieu, this justice identified "a lack of knowledge about oneself, a kind of emotional immaturity." These psychological factors might lead to neither understanding one's own emotions (especially negative ones) nor the consequences of one's own decisions. Hence, he added, "the range of empathy is blocked." Almost identical reasons were articulated by another judge [9], who highlighted a problem with being overly empathic and the lack of "an ability to deal with one's own emotions and recognize them. This is a general problem of emotional intelligence." Another judge [20] emphasized a lack of sufficient distance. It is hard for some people to endure emotions stemming from their empathy and simultaneously maintain proper balance.

Spotlighting an additional factor, a criminal division justice [14] with over a dozen years of experience emphasized professional development and the augmentation of professional skills, especially with respect to leadership qualities. According to this woman, judicial leaders with little knowledge about managing people and organizational processes can introduce organizational chaos and disorder. Leadership style can greatly affect the strength of an organizational culture, which, consequently, directly influences the quality of interactions and relationships within that environment. Thus, nonempathetic leaders might lead not only to the decline of the judicial system's organizational culture but also nonempathic behavior among judges. In a similar vein, a judge [12] stressed the wide range of responsibilities of judges that extend beyond courtroom work, such as various administrative activities, which might dull an empathic acumen. Somewhat linked to that factor have been general changes taking place in the Polish judiciary—especially the direction of reforms being introduced at the time we were conducting our empirical research. A judge [6] lamented: "This is what I worry about, but today's situation of courts and judges does not favor empathy and does not at all favor the understanding of the role of empathy; today we [are going in] a completely different direction."

Overall, empathy is crucial for fair and effective judicial decision-making, but its application is often curtailed by entrenched attitudes, organizational pressures, and systemic challenges. Addressing these obstacles involves promoting continuous self-reflection, professional development, and systemic changes that prioritize the humane aspects of judicial work.

Should a judge be empathic or not?

Initial findings

As described earlier, our strategy was based on a decision not to begin interviewing with a direct inquiry about empathy in judicial labor. Instead, we presented some opening themes, leading to empathy being referenced in the judicial context. Only as we approached the end of the conversation did we introduce a normative question aimed at expanding and summarizing the views the judges in our sample held about empathy in the judicial context. That question in the final stage of the interview was general in nature, allowing for more spontaneous remarks. The query was also formulated alternatively—whether judges should or should not be empathetic. This approach was designed to create the possibility of opening, limiting, or even neglecting the role of empathy in the judicial process. Essentially, we hoped to elicit justifications for or against the desirability of empathy in this context. The aim was to bring to light a fuller spectrum of themes judges might raise in response; this would inform us about their ways of thinking with regard to the prescribed place of empathy in judicial decision-making. Additionally, we expected this question to provide material supplementing their answers to the more concrete questions, thus enriching our comprehension of their perspectives on empathy in their judicial roles.

Crucially, all the judges responded affirmatively to the question of whether judges should be empathetic. There were no attempts to completely dismiss a prescriptive role of empathy in judicial labor. Nevertheless, and unsurprisingly, the level of enthusiasm in the formulations of their favorable answers did vary, as did the details and comprehensiveness of the justifications for this general claim. Moreover, in answering this question, the majority of judges emphasized the need for limits to the utilization of empathy and outlined certain conditions for its use. Empathy was not presented as universally desirable or a silver bullet that would unconditionally resolve the problems of the judiciary. Our interviewees mostly provided much more insight into the scope and variety of reasons for limiting empathy in judicial decision-making than for employing it—the former was easier for them to articulate than the latter.

Given the overrepresentation of voices advocating for limitations, one might wonder whether this affirmation of the need for empathetic judges was influenced by the difficulty of stating that "judges should not be empathetic" when empathy is a socially valued concept. It might also be that judges, for various reasons, are not accustomed to fleshing out their thoughts on this. In any case, their attempts to isolate and delimit the role of empathy is, to some degree, expected, since judges typically try to navigate between different requirements and would thus try to situate empathy among other components of their role. Finally, mentioning boundaries is also not unexpected, considering the biases that (easy) empathy could bring to judgments. The boundaries drawn by the judges in our sample differ in nature and scope, but the emerging zones can be classified into a few categories.

Limitations on using empathy

First of all, certain limitations on the intensity and scope of using empathy, according to some judges, correlate with the well-being of the decision-maker. This line of thinking stresses that empathizing is demanding and, when employed without limits, it can negatively impact conditions. Several judges mentioned that uncontrolled empathy could be detrimental not only to the judges themselves but also to their effectiveness in handling cases and interacting with other participants. This perspective is particularly interesting because the literature rarely emphasizes the limits of using empathy by judges in terms of their own psychological well-being.

One interviewee [12] expressed that "the judge should be empathic, but not too much, I would say. [The judge] should not go too far in this empathizing. . . . [The judge] should not put too much feeling into the situation of the parties because that leads to professional burnout." The process of "getting into" leads to being overwhelmed by others' problems, decisions, and misfortunes and, if too intense, corrupts a judge's well-being. In a similar vein, another judge [15] who acknowledged some positive functions of empathy also mentioned that "on the other hand, empathy disturbs the judge for sure as it leads to an emotional burden." This is especially true when empathizing closely resembles emotional involvement. Another judge [8], while mentioning other boundaries, highlighted that "the excessive entering into someone's shoes or investigation of motivation . . . can be tiring." Thus, not only affective empathy but also cognitive empathy can be seen by judges as precipitating a negative state upon themselves. Interestingly, one judge [23] differentiated between negative ("devastating") feelings when empathizing with one type of participant—child victims. Doing this "would discharge my batteries very fast. And I try to approach it professionally and try not to get into these emotions too much." This getting into the children was also interpreted as corrupting the ability to be objective. Here, the threat to the profession is emphasized: Empathizing with certain parties could very negatively influence the decision-maker and the decision-making process. Yet too much empathy also constitutes a personal problem for a judge. Asked about what "too much" meant, she clarified that it would be "feeling other's states"—something that links to emotional contagion. Thus, the judges objected to an unconditional use of easy empathy.

Second, several judges stressed that only the existence of certain situational factors justifies the need for empathy. This line of thinking spotlights the limited spheres in which empathy is welcomed—which presupposes that in all others it is at least problematic. Considering both being empathic while also showing it to others, one judge [1] believed that, generally speaking, judges should be empathetic, but "it depends on the situation—in some situations they should, but in others, absolutely not." Later he presented a slightly amended view when he acknowledged that judges should be empathic inside, and this was his case, but still, "there is . . . the issue of how [they] can show [empathy] in certain situations." Unfortunately, he did not provide clear guidance on how to differentiate the situations in which showing empathy is desirable and when it is unnecessary.

For another judge [29], features such as "the nature of the case, the parties, [and] the involvement of professional representatives" have some bearing on the legitimacy of empathy. Unfortunately, we do not know what these three categories designate exactly and how using them would look in practice. Referring to the first criterion, a former civil division judge [23] argued that, in simpler cases, there is no space for the use of empathy: "What would

I do with empathy when, I don't know, she bought some stuff and didn't pay for it. . . . The facts are just as they are: she did not pay, so she is going to pay." Such easy cases were contrasted with family or criminal cases, in which "empathy plays a much more important role . . . as it is more important here to imagine people's emotions."

A judge [4] presiding in criminal cases began by stressing the boundaries of utilizing empathy: "[Judges] should be empathetic—this is without a doubt for me—but to a limited extent. This empathy cannot be [used often] as in our daily life. We have these boundaries that result from the nature of the job, but, wherever possible, and, to some extent, empathy should be absolutely shown by us." The "nature of the [judicial] job" defines a general boundary of using, or rather showing, empathy. Asked about the exceptional situations in which empathy should be welcomed, our interviewees clarified that this applies to big cases, where there is a concentration of contacts between the judge and the accused and/or victims. In such cases, there is more space for a better understanding of the reactions of participants, and thus empathy is more needed. This presupposes the role of empathy in managing the interactional realm in courtrooms.

Third, several judges stressed that something that activates the emotionality associated with empathy is tantamount to a robust limit to its use. In line with what the judicial dispassion script dictates, these judges recognized, or at least communicated, a need for empathy in their work, but definitively and without sentiment. Many judges emphasized that empathy-related, unlimited, uncontrolled emotionality constitutes a boundary against its use. One participant [24] stated that a judge "should be [empathetic], but must keep it in check, control it, and not succumb to it. Understand the parties, the situation, yes, but [one] must keep feelings in check and be guided by law and logic. But [one] should not be blind, Themis should not be completely blind: she should listen to emotions but control the susceptibility to empathy. Impose a muzzle, but not suppress it . . . but have those feelings—and they should influence the decision." This judge relied on the assumed tension between emotions and reason and placed empathy in the realm of the former, which immediately restricts its use, although, interestingly, it does not imply its necessary elimination. In a similar vein, another judge [2] stated that "One must be careful with empathy. This means that one cannot allow emotions to regain control." Another judge [34] underscored that "I am not an automaton," adding that "[a judge] should have empathy but not emotionality and should not use emotional expressions, because it can lead to accusations of bias." Another interesting position was taken by a judge [18] who remarked that "an excess of empathy does not help in resolving a case . . . [but] this does not mean that the court should not be empathetic, because a certain note of emotionality should still be present inside. But an excess . . . I would rather lean toward minimization, yes, maybe that's my answer." What is this "note of emotionality" supposed to be? Continuing, the judge pointed to the inalienability of emotions, which is "natural for people, I think, and there is no way to protect oneself from them."

Fourth, according to some judges, minimizing the role of empathy is justified by the necessity to protect the fundamental values of the judiciary (e.g., objectivity, impartiality), which are at risk when there is too much empathy. One judge [23] explained that "when I overly identify with these human problems and feel them as my own and start getting lost, it distorts objectivity in the given situation the most." This judge also commented that "emotions are present on both sides . . . I don't see such a schizophrenic situation where I feel the emotions of both sides equally. Most often, I suppose, I would identify with one of the sides and this would prevent me from objectively assessing the situation." This leads to the conclusion that "an appropriate level of empathy is needed, but not too much. Too much [empathy] causes trouble." Significantly, this judge rejected the possibility of a symmetrical distribution of empathy toward the parties. Another participant [34] stated that a judge "should have empathy, but not emotionality and not use emotional expressions, because it can lead to accusations of bias." In this view, too much empathy, laden with emotion, causes judges to be perceived as biased. Interestingly, this person did not consider that judges might actually be biased regardless of empathy. Another judge [15] also developed this motif of empathy boundaries being exceeded and thus leading to accusations of prejudice: She treated "accusations of bias" as negative not because they disrupt judicial decision-making, but precisely because "they harm a judge's reputation."

The next example refers to identification with someone associated with an empathy that leads to a loss of objectivity. Although this judge [20] expressed a positive view about the need for empathy, he clarified his definition of the term:

> [I see empathy] as a willingness to cooperate, an understanding of the other person, but not compassion and the full entering into their role. Because if we put [ourselves] into someone's role—although only, let me say, experimentally, to put [ourselves] into the place of this person whom we access in order to assess—this could be dangerous, because we could identify too much with this person. And the objectivity can be corrupted. I am trying not to enter the shoes of this person . . . because when I enter the shoes of one person, and then I enter the other's, then I do not know in which shoes I feel more comfortable. Thus, for sure the understanding is what we need, but not identification.

Another perspective was provided by a judge [21] who emphasized the risks associated with using empathy in the courtroom, specifically when parties try to exploit it. The judge warned that such manipulation could undermine key procedural values, stating, "A gentleman comes with crutches, but it turns out that, a few days ago, he was carrying a flag for three hours during a [demonstration]. . . . We need to keep empathy and compassion on a leash because we cannot allow ourselves to be swayed. . . . We might lean too far toward one person and ignore what the evidence tells us." This highlights that unchecked empathy, especially the more superficial or easy form, can distort the trial process, enabling manipulative practices by participants and overshadowing the importance of solid evidence.

Arguments for judges being empathic

Although the judges in our sample unanimously agreed that empathy should be part of a judge's repertoire, their focus was on the boundaries of its jurisdiction, rather than on substantiations for this position. Nonetheless, a few pathways toward validation and justification in this regard can be identified.

First, certain judges referred to the humanization and de-mechanization of the process as positive and desirable states that can be achieved through the use of empathy. In this case, empathy changes the judicial process. According to this view, one participant [5] stated that judges "should be [empathetic] because, in adjudicating and applying the law in specific situations, we deal with people. Norms alone do not decide everything, and the way we apply the law is an important element of the judiciary." In like manner, another participant [23] stated that "judges should be empathetic because applying the law is not applying dry norms." She then emphasized the educational dimension of the process and that "an unempathetic judge is not suited to this profession." Another judge [16] admitted that "we should have a humanistic perspective on the situation, not just based on the law." Another judge [17] argued that "without empathy, we would be a machine for issuing judgments. . . . Law is a system, but law is [also] people." Another example is the view of a judge [20] who said that "empathy, properly understood, is needed for judges, whether criminal, civil, or family. He works with people . . . but the problems are related to humans, and he must understand them." Empathy is a set of competencies that work to safeguard what may be lost through the "mechanicalness" of procedures.

Second, judges do see the positive role that empathy plays and should play in gathering or evaluating evidence and in establishing the facts necessary for decision-making. One judge [16] pointed out the role of empathy in assessing the credibility of the people being heard and in the ability to reconstruct not only "what someone said, but what they wanted to say." In a similar vein, another judge [13] pointed to the desirable role of empathy in evaluating evidence, especially witness testimony. This was echoed by a criminal court judge [12], who admitted that judges should be empathetic, "because this trait allows him to put himself in the position of the party, to understand [them]. And if we understand both sides, it will be much easier to issue a fair judgment with the same evidence compared to a situation without empathy." Other judges also touched on this topic. One of them [15] justified the assertion that judges should be empathetic by referring to the fact that it allows them to better understand the parties, their motivations, reasons for claims, and relationships between the parties. Using empathy in all these contexts, according to the judge, ultimately helps in issuing better judgments. A family court judge [3] noted that justices "should be empathetic to understand the other side and the motives behind behavior. . . . If we do not have empathy, how are we to assess participants—because it is impossible to use one template for everyone, and each person is a separate individual, each has unique experiences." Empathy responds to this pluralism and individualism in the human world, enabling a better understanding of the factual basis of a case.

Third, certain judges indicated that empathy helps achieve rhetorical goals or contributes to procedural justice. The term "rhetorical goals" refers to activities aimed at convincing or ensuring that the parties or participants received proper attention and were taken into account. For one judge [13], "cold logic, reason, and linguistic analysis do not allow for ensuring justice. Especially convincing [others] that this judgment was fair. It's about creating the impression in the addressees that it was [fair] . . . showing that we considered the motivation, took it into account, and considered the parties' claims." The main function of empathy, according to the judge, is to create certain impressions on the participants in the judicial process. Similarly, another judge [6] referred to the social legitimacy of the judicial apparatus, which is based on a "mechanism of mutual reinforcement." The judge pointed out the importance of "the feeling that [litigants] were heard and treated with attention, which is crucial for acceptance of the system's operation." From this perspective, empathy is a skill that helps judges justify such impressions. The use of empathy—a judge's attempt to understand the situation of the parties concerned and consider their hypothetical narrative from their perspective—was placed in the context of concern for legitimacy, understood correspondingly to the voice criterion in the literature on procedural justice.

Lastly, another line of thinking emphasizes that empathy should be used by decision-makers because it provides something important, as it helps cultivate needed attitudes and brings job satisfaction. One judge [8], while also pointing out the limitations of empathy, simultaneously admitted that "[a judge] should not be completely closed off—because this is a profession where sympathy for people is needed and being empathetic helps in doing this job . . . [and then] satisfaction is greater." In a like manner, another judge [9] justified the need to use empathy by emphasizing that it provides "greater satisfaction with the judgment and the parties' reaction—gratitude that I thought it through, listened, and imposed obligations that are not detached from their reality, but not mine." The importance of empathy for the decision-maker was mentioned by a judge [6] who emphasized that it is needed for "self-acceptance for what I do." The judge explained that "For me, empathy is needed to feel good in this whole situation, not to feel that I am just an official." In these cases, judges indicated that empathy brings something important to the decision-makers themselves.

Summary

The opinions of the interviewees in our sample regarding the issue of whether judges should be empathetic led to several overall reflections. First, judges seem to lack a deeply thought-out and justified vision of the desired areas and ways of using empathy in the decision-making process. However, in statements remaining at a descriptive level and referring to their own experiences, the justices in our cohort pointed out many more benefits pertaining to empathy at various stages of their decision-making process. In a sense, it can be said that these judges spoke in verse: That is, without using the term itself, they described practices that perfectly fit within the framework of judicial empathy. They pointed out, for example, anticipating the reactions of people in the courtroom and using a range of verbal and nonverbal behaviors (e.g., greeting parties in family cases with a smile, warm gestures, encouragement, verbal communication); they indicated an understanding of the participants' situations or directly adopted the perspectives of others.

Second, it is striking that judges, when asked "should judges be empathetic or not," rarely pointed to the range of cognitive limitations (found in the specialized literature) associated with uncontrolled and untrained empathizing (e.g., familiarity bias, similarity bias, here-and-now bias). The interviewed justices generally seemed to pay more attention to being perceived as partial than to controlling their own cognitive processes (including easy empathy) so as to be more truly impartial. Third, it is interesting that, for some judges, empathy poses a threat to their psychological well-being, while for others, it is necessary to humanize and give meaning to their work. In both cases, the use of empathy does impact (though fundamentally differently) the well-being of these decision-makers themselves—something that brings new insight into considerations of judicial empathy.

Conclusions

The objective of our thematic approach during the data analysis was to create a preliminary map of judges' views and experiences regarding empathy in their work. This chapter has presented a general overview, emphasizing the complexity and diversity of the perspectives unveiled here. The methodological challenges of studying the views of judges with respect to empathy are particularly weighty. Among other things, asking judges (more or less directly) about empathy introduces its own limitations, which are amplified by the elusiveness of empathy and its somewhat problematic nature within traditional judicial culture.

Despite these challenges, dismissal of judges' standpoints on empathy would hamper comprehensive understanding of the part justices themselves play in this. Even though the sample could not be fully representative, the main finding is both intriguing and somewhat surprising: Judges largely expressed positive views about empathy's role in their work and responded affirmatively to the question of whether judges should be empathetic.

The judges with whom we spoke identified several points in the decision-making process at which they employ empathy. That decision-making encompasses a range of processes from perspective-taking to emotional tuning. Certain responses were unexpected, such as the strong emphasis on using empathy during the oral justification of rulings. Interestingly, the contexts in which the judges claimed to use empathy were broader than the limited scope typically mentioned when discussing empathy's formal role in judicial work.

This discrepancy may be explained by the challenges judges face when discussing empathy in the judicial context, as well as by their lack of reflexivity regarding the role of soft skills in their work. When asked directly whether judges should be empathetic, they often had less to say than when discussing more concrete aspects of their role without explicitly using the word. This suggests that empathy, though underdiscussed, plays a more significant role in judicial practice than judges themselves may consciously recognize.

References

Avgoustinos, Costa. 2007 "The Compassionate Judge." *Public Space: The Journal of Law and Social Justice* 1: 1–41.

Bandes, Susan A. 1996. "Empathy, Narrative, and Victim Impact Statements." *University of Chicago Law Review* 63: 361–412.

Bandes, Susan A. 2017. "Compassion and the Rule of Law." *International Journal of Law in Context* 13(2): 184–196.

Bergman Blix, Stina and Åsa Wettergren. 2018. *Professional Emotions in Court: A Sociological Perspective.* London and New York: Routledge.

Bladini, Moa and Stina Bergman Blix. 2022. "The Judge Under Pressure: Fostering Objectivity by Abandoning the Myth of Dispassion." In *Judicial Independence Under Threat*, edited by Dimitrios Giannoulopoulos and Yvonne McDermott. London: Oxford University Press.

Chin, Denny. 2012. "Sentencing: A Role for Empathy." *University of Pennsylvania Law Review* 160: 1561–1584.

Cormack, Warren. 2021. "Reassessing the Judicial Empathy Debate: How Empathy Can Distort and Improve Criminal Sentencing." *Mitchell Hamline Law Review* 47(4): 81–110.

Del Mar, Maksymilian. 2017 "Imagining by Feeling: A Case for Compassion in Legal Reasoning." *International Journal of Law in Context* 13(2): 143–157.

Dudek, Michał and Mateusz Stępień. 2021. *Power Distance Courtroom Dynamics.* Cham: Springer.

Hochschild, Arlie. 1983. *The Managed Heart: Commercialization of Human Feeling.* Berkley: University of California Press.

Kosior, Wojciech and Jakub Łukasiewicz. 2018. *Family Law in Poland.* Rzeszów: Legal Publishing House. https://open.icm.edu.pl/server/api/core/bitstreams/04cf4e81-a243-4fbc-aa09-fdbbbecd1ef4/content

Maroney, Terry A. 2011. "The Persistent Cultural Script of Judicial Dispassion." *California Law Review* 99: 629–681.

Maroney, Terry and Phillip Ackerman-Lieberman. 2014. "As a Father Shows Compassion for His Children." *Journal of Law, Religion and State* 2(3): 240–275.

Posner, Richard A. 2013. *Reflections of Judging.* Cambridge, MA: Harvard University Press.

Stępień, Mateusz. 2021. "On the Relationship between Judicial Empathy and the Integrity of Judges." *Krytyka Prawa. Niezależne Studia Nad Prawem* 13(3): 98–113.

Tyler, Tom R. 2000. "Social Justice: Outcome and Procedure." *International Journal of Psychology* 35: 117–125.

Zipursky, Benjamin. 1990. "*DeShaney* and the Jurisprudence of Compassion." *New York University Law Review* 65: 1101–1147.

5 Empathy and impartiality

"Friends" or "foes"?

Mateusz Stępień

Introduction

The relationship between empathy and impartiality in the judicial context is central to debates in both legal scholarship and public discourse. Because of the importance and complexity of this issue, it was treated as a separate topic during empirical research, with findings discussed individually. This separation was also necessary because empathy and impartiality evoke strong emotions and are subjects of interest among many, sparking intense debates. Some claim that empathy and impartiality are "foes," while others see them as "friends." For the first group, a judge's empathy introduces biases, unequal treatment of parties, or the impact of emotions into the decision-making process. All these factors ostensibly corrupt impartiality. Their opponents, however, suggest that empathy does not disrupt impartiality and can even help secure it, as empathy allows judges to transcend their own perspectives and debias themselves (see Franks 2011; Colby 2012; Lee 2014; Maibom 2022: Chapter 10). In addition to the scholarly debates, and as already underscored in this volume, public discourse debates also arose (not only in the United States) in reaction to Barack Obama's emphasis on the empathy factor in judicial appointments (see West 2011; Fissell 2016; see also Zipursky 2012). On the one hand, the issue triggered a wave of criticism; on the other, there were voices in support of Obama, discerning empathy's positive impact on the judiciary.

Certainly, delving into how judges read the juxtaposition also raises the issue of their understanding of both empathy and impartiality. As previously noted, views on empathy held by judges themselves had not been gathered and analyzed before our undertaking of the extensive research project whose outcomes constitute the keystone of this book. Regarding impartiality, it is remarkable that the literature has not (with rare exceptions) provided substantial insight into how justices see its meaning and significance (e.g., Mack et al. 2021; Roach Anleu, Mack 2021: 67–70). In fact, our project did not foresee novel and keen insights into impartiality, yet the research unexpectedly brought to light a number of intriguing, relevant tropes. With this knowledge in mind, it became feasible to reconstruct judges' opinions about the correlation between empathy and impartiality. Taking the next step forward, this

DOI: 10.4324/9781003546580-6

chapter poses the question: In the judges' eyes, what correspondence do they discern between using empathy and securing impartiality? Of particular interest will be whether they see empathy as a factor supporting or undermining impartiality.

Recalling that only when bringing the interview to a close did we query the judges about the empathy-impartiality relationship, and our strategy was rewarded by a willingness to reflect upon yet another matter, while avoiding too easily formulated opinions. With the interview guide taking judges naturally through their general understandings of empathy articulated at the outset and then their discussions of empathy-related themes in the judicial context specifically, the concluding conversation about empathy's interaction with impartiality likely constituted a holistic compendium. Simply put, how judges understand empathy is of consequence in how they see its interactions with impartiality. Certain judges underscored empathy's emotional aspect (e.g., co-feeling, getting into, feeling with), while others emphasized it as a cognitive process, focusing on understanding others' situations and perspectives without necessarily sharing their emotions. Still, a few judges introduced unique angles that shed light on empathy's role not only in understanding others but also in fostering collaboration and mutual respect. This is not only less controversial when applied to the judicial domain but also appears to align with judicial values and may even be seen as a means of ensuring, rather than undermining, impartiality. That said, more fruitful at this point would be to focus on the overarching tendencies, dominant themes, and types of approaches that judges have employed. A broader analysis can bring more knowledge about attitudes within the judicial community regarding key aspects of judicial decision-making.

A main finding: empathy and impartiality are not enemies

A noteworthy discovery from the study is that all of the interviewed judges perceived no fundamental contradiction between practicing empathy and upholding impartiality. In their collective opinion, an empathetic judge can still be impartial. However, this conclusion encompasses various reasons that justify the coexistence of both empathy and impartiality. The research identifies five main strategies employed by judges to reconcile empathy with impartiality, shedding light on the nuanced ways judges navigate this intersection in their decision-making processes.

The first strategy is based on the idea of symmetry in empathy distribution between parties. The view that empathy is not injurious if it is equally dispersed between both sides emphasizes the formal requirement of treating all parties equally. The second strategy defines empathy as unemotional: When emotionality is excluded, empathy (more closely associated with reason) does not threaten impartiality. The third approach involves mitigating empathy's influence on judgments: When empathy's reach does not extend to the final decision, it is considered harmless. The fourth strategy emphasizes control over empathy, ensuring that it does not lead to excesses or negative consequences.

This approach assumes that empathy is unavoidable, but the key is to control and monitor it rather than deny its existence. The final strategy, which is somewhat more radical, prioritizes empathy, allowing for its broader application by de-emphasizing strict formal impartiality. These five strategies will be presented in detail with pertinent commentary. Kept in mind is that each strategy has its own internal problems and unresolved controversies—this, too, will be discussed. Furthermore, noteworthy is that judges often combine two or even three of these strategies by way of reconciling empathy and impartiality as they formulate their opinions.

To fully understand the key findings, it is also important to consider how judges conceptualize impartiality vis-à-vis their earlier presented verbalizations of how they understand empathy. Investigating judges' perceptions of impartiality is crucial for a better grasp of why they do not discern a fundamental incongruity between empathy and impartiality. It may be that specific definitions and interpretations of impartiality alter the perception of its compatibility with empathy.

Judges' understanding of impartiality

The understandings of impartiality expressed by judges in our sample vary; they are also generally not as sophisticated as one might expect, considering the weight placed on this in the judicial sphere. Many judges seem to view impartiality as a noncontroversial matter, relying on tacit knowledge to guide their thoughts about it. Only a few judges strove to articulate their understanding of impartiality, rather than treat it as self-explanatory. In typical interpretations, impartiality was equated with "non-favoritism" [37] or "seeing the interests of both sides" [30].

The majority explored and cared more about external impartiality, ensuring that a judge is not perceived by others as biased or prejudiced. In this case, an emphasis is placed on how judicial behavior, decisions, words, and gestures are seen by others, but not on the ongoing and varied processes taking place inside the judges themselves (see Roach Anleu, Mack 2017: 9). Thus, justices marginalize internal impartiality, which focuses on both exploring the actual reasons for a decision and considering the processes occurring inside the decision-maker while reaching a final decision.

Interestingly, Stina Bergman Blix and Asa Wettergren highlighted situations in which judges used empathy—particularly when assessing their "appearance of impartiality from the perspective of the defendant" (2016: 35). However, such an evaluation—often driven by established cognitive scripts and ready-to-use associations—may not constitute genuine empathy. In these instances, judges rely on certain cues and establish truths by which to gauge how they are perceived. Nonetheless, the assumption is insufficiently supported for this phenomenon to be accepted as true empathy.

Leaving this issue aside, the interview transcripts are full of examples of an external approach to impartiality. One judge [13] expressed the view that "we [judges] should secure impartiality. . . . This should be stressed and manifested at each step, that we are not on any side." This justice strongly emphasized the importance of continuously demonstrating impartiality. Another judge [29] similarly emphasized that "I have to be very careful not to violate this principle of impartiality in [someone's] perception, because someone can perceive my actions as partial." Regarding the use of empathy, this judge candidly admitted, "I do not always see the need [for using it] and not always do I have measures [to apply it]. . . . But I must be very conscious and careful, in order not to violate the principle of impartiality in perception, in perception [of others], because my actions can be read as partial." Relevantly, ensuring an external impartiality may require not showing empathy—or at least not showing it in a way that could be interpreted as partial—though this does not necessarily mean the judge lacks empathy.

Some judges rely heavily on idealistic considerations, grounded in legal requirements that assume justices to be inherently impartial. For these judges, achieving impartiality is not viewed as a task that requires effort, work, or deep consideration; rather, it is seen as intrinsic to the judicial role. This perspective leads them to dismiss the notion that they could ever be anything but impartial. From this standpoint, judicial impartiality is treated as an unchangeable given, and, consequently, empathy is nonproblematic, since it is incapable of altering the assumed default state. Fortunately, a number of justices in our sample did see impartiality as a distinct process, a kind of internal labor (in contrast with surface acting; see Mack, Roach Anleu 2010). Consequently, novel topics and tensions were identified, and the establishment of impartiality was seen as actual work that judges must undertake. Looking at impartiality this way involves two positions.

According to the first, impartiality is a state relatively easy to achieve for the judge (e.g., simply maintaining a poker face). Few were the justices who adhered to the easy empathy thesis. Nevertheless, one judge [26] expressed a similar view while discussing the human face, acknowledging that, despite expressing a kind demeanor in the courtroom, "there is a need not to make room for the feelings of the parties, that the side of one party is being taken"; key here is that this judge added "this is not so hard [to do]." To be noted is that this judge remained in the domain of external impartiality. Easy empathy work does not imply that empathic impulses are necessarily destructive, since it is a straightforward thing to at least present oneself as impartial. But this does not tell us how empathy influences the judge.

The second approach is based on a more realistic representation of the decision-making process: It acknowledges the difficulty of achieving absolute impartiality but avoids the meaninglessness of attempts to achieve it. As this position implies, impartiality is an impossible state to fully achieve, even with the use of certain tools by judges and the presence of certain institutional conditions. Jeffrey M. Shaman substituted "difficulty" with the assertion that "pure impartiality is an ideal that can never be completely attained" (1996: 605). Most interviewees stressed this difficulty.

One judge [14] argued that absolute impartiality is a utopia, as "everyone is shaped, has some opinions, ethical and moral, something for him is good and bad. . . . Talking about absolute impartiality . . . there is no chance." Some shared their deeper observations during the interview. A justice [20] admitted that "everyone is subjective: it is not true that everyone is objective. And the judges are not an exception. However, [they] must tend to look as objective as possible, and consider circumstances that could corrupt that objectivity." In some sense, the subjectivity of justices cannot be eliminated, and the only thing that can be done is to be perceived as objective. Another judge [29] mentioned that "I am always tending to be impartial, however, this is hard, because the heart often whispers something different." That statement accentuates the need for internal work on the heartfelt impulses. Here, putatively, empathy could assist the decision-maker in this endeavor by enhancing the reflexive grasping of one's own perspective by taking that of the other.

A focus on the external view of impartiality often aligns with the belief that judges are integrally impartial due to their professionalism, extensive education, and ethical standards. From this standpoint, the emphasis is placed on managing others' perceptions of the judges, rather than on examining the internal processes that could ensure impartiality. In accord with this approach, empathy is not seen as a threat to true impartiality; instead, empathy is viewed as a potential problem and not only in terms of how it might be seen by others. The strategy, therefore, may involve not displaying empathy in order to maintain the appearance of impartiality, which is seen as or assumed to be a safer approach. This perspective does not consider the actual impact of empathy on judicial decisions. Such a view on impartiality may contribute to a judge's failure to perceive a conflict between empathy and impartiality. Again, if impartiality is seen as an inherent quality, rather than an active, managed state, then empathy's role in decision-making is less likely to be seen as problematic.

Five reconciliation strategies

Symmetry in distributing empathy between parties

With regard to the first pathway by which judges have attempted to reconcile empathy with impartiality, the latter is maintained when the former is directed equally toward all participants involved in a case. In other words, empathy does not compromise a judge's impartiality as long as it is applied fairly and uniformly; there is no innate contradiction between the two as long as all receive similar understanding and consideration, or if their situations are approached with equal depth of feeling. Such a position is described in the literature by, among others, Thomas Colby (2012: 1946), who defined the "ideal empathic judge" as one who "has a talent for empathy and makes a conscious effort to empathize with all parties, thus ensuring that she is not subconsciously undervaluing the interests of those whose perspectives she does not instinctively appreciate."

Several of the judges interviewed for our research supported this "symmetry thesis," but emphasized the challenges in achieving equal empathy distribution. As one judge [18] stated, only if one is "empathic to both parties [can I] secure impartiality." However, this is not an easy task and "can bring a negative outcome, thus [judges should use empathy] with moderation." Another interviewee [14] concurred that genuine empathy extends to all parties, suggesting that its management is necessary to ensure even allotment. The next judge [33] also adhered to the symmetry thesis, affirming that true impartiality arises when a judge behaves "empathically in the same way toward both parties." Arguing that emotions and personal worldviews must be set aside, she reinforced that a conscious effort is required to suppress inclinations stemming from an emotional connection or shared values with one of the parties in a case. Thus, the symmetry thesis not only implies evenly balanced empathy but also simultaneous, fair-minded blocking of other emotional responses.

Importantly, some judges—even if starting from the symmetry thesis—subjected it to criticism. One judge [36] opened with an observation that "a lot of judges would say 'no' [to the thesis that the empathic judge can be simultaneously impartial]"—an assessment not corroborated in our sample. Nonetheless, he later pondered the possibility that "empathy would be applied to all participants in the same way." Yet dwelling on this, he imagined a case in which "We have a crying lady, and the other does not cry, and we would say 'I understand your situation.'" That, in his opinion, would undermine impartiality. Another example he provided considered a civil case between a private person and a company with legal standing but questions "how to be empathic toward the company." Extrapolating, the symmetry thesis appears simple and promising, but the real dynamics of hearings and the logic of a judicial trial render it problematic.

Other judges, representing different views, pointed out weaknesses in the symmetry thesis. One judge [32] argued that impartiality cannot constitute some undeviating behavior or demeanor, while another [23] likened the attempt to feel the same toward both sides to a "schizophrenic endeavor" (likely resulting in something akin to easy empathy). Additionally, another interviewee [31] noted that the behavior and reactions of other participants in the courtroom contribute to shaping a space in which empathy could be applied by justices. In certain situations, judges may find it challenging to employ empathy due to factors such as a lack of cooperation from even one party. This suggests that an actual, symmetrical application of empathy is dependent on other factors and not everything is always possible.

All in all, the symmetry thesis, though often recalled in the interviews, was also critiqued. In general, upholding that thesis is an easy way to make empathy and impartiality seem to be friends, but, in fact, the strategy likely only superficially resolves the empathy-impartiality problem: A formal equality is easy to accept in theory, but hard to apply due to a plethora of issues and subtleties. As Kathy Mack et al. (2021: 21) correctly asserted, "empathy is not a zero-sum game; each party's need for judicial empathy may be different."

Defining empathy as unemotional

The next strategy for defending a correspondence (or at least the absence of conflict) between empathy and impartiality in the courtroom involves a definition of empathy that sidelines or eliminates any perceived conflict. This approach gives prominence to a more cognitive comprehension of someone's circumstances, rather than to an emotional engagement. In contrast to definitions that include emotional components and are seen as imperiling impartiality (Maroney, Ackerman-Lieberman 2014: 246), authors who argue that empathy is not bias-generating adopt definitions of empathy that draw attention to "understanding the perspective of others" without emotional resonance (Lee 2014: 152). Although the professional culture of the judiciary traditionally portrays emotions as irritants in the decision-making process, this view is evolving, as seen in the growing influence of the law and emotion movement even in Poland (Wojciechowski et al. 2015). By defining empathy in terms of cognitive understanding rather than emotional involvement, judges can reconcile its use with their commitment to impartiality.

Archetypal in this regard is a statement by one of the judges [25] for whom "an empathic judge can be impartial, empathy that means understanding the position of the other side, but [at the same time] acknowledging a given legal context." Not only the cognitive side is accentuated but also a requirement that empathy not be the sole determinant of the decision. Similarly, another judge [34], in line with his view of empathy as being responsive, noticed that "when a judge is sensitive to the needs of others, and is not driven by emotions, and does not tilt the scale toward some party, [he] can be impartial. No one is a machine." Here a slip into emotionality is risky, but empathy as a sensitivity does not invite serious problems.

Another example is quite telling: A family judge [27] argued that "because empathy does not assume that we are surely going to get into [someone], but that we are going to understand the situation of one party, [and] only empathy allows for understanding the situation of both sides—thus, we are not losing the impartiality." The last part of this obviously refers to the symmetry thesis. Later on the judge admitted that "It is not a case of one getting into the role of this person, this mother, this father, but empathy would allow us to maybe understand the situation of this person—why she acts this way, what her legal claim [was] raised for—but not getting into her role." Intriguing is a shift in this family court judge's reasoning: her approach to empathy at the beginning of the interview encompassed the getting-into, but, to fit the argument, she changed from an emotionally saturated description of empathy to one more reason based (a better fit with impartiality).

Certainly, in these instances, when addressing matters related to impartiality, there seems to be a concerted effort to refine definitions of empathy, detaching emotionality from judging. Consequently, these judges from our sample appeared to gravitate toward equating empathy with a safer option. Yet noteworthy is how some seemed to adjust their conception of empathy over the course of the interview itself: The subject of impartiality drove them to align more closely with perspective-taking, with cognitive rather than affective empathy. Such instances of a real-time, subconscious modification during the interview could be interpreted as a means of anchoring the image of judicial professionalism and dispassion (see Maroney 2011).

Mitigating empathy's influence on judicial decisions

A different pathway toward reconciling empathy with impartiality involves strongly underscoring that a judge's empathy does not impinge upon the reaching of a final decision. That culmination—the most important stage of a court case—is presented as free of the troubles and dilemmas that empathy (especially selective, partial, or strongly affective empathy) brings. According to this line of thinking, empathy is pictured as a competency functioning in earlier phases of judicial decision-making. Factored into this are views that empathy can be channeled at previous stages and set aside, or that it is just not used by judges in decision-making. This argument was most often mentioned by the judges in our sample and finds its representation in the literature. For example, Susan Bandes (1996: 379) claims that understanding of a defendant's perspective does not mean "absolving him of responsibility." Bandes (2017: 185) expands on this by avowing that "judges may feel empathy for all litigants before her. It is her job to understand what is at stake for the parties. Once she has done so, she must make a legal determination about which side prevails."

Exploring this avenue, a judge [35] elucidated: "I can understand both parties, but I will pass a judgment which I think is just." Harking back to the symmetry thesis, this judge stated that, ultimately, her decisions were not driven by empathy, but by other factors. Similarly, another judge [30] admitted that "the feeling informs [the proceedings], but rationality is what decides." Further, another interviewee [28] firmly stated that "the judgment is based on evidence and within the limits of the law. Empathy helps, but it is one element—empathy helps in questioning, contacts with people." Echoing this view, a judge [17] acknowledged that all people possess some kind of empathy and "I could be empathic to an old lady, but if her testimony does not fit the other material and appears not to be true, then I won't decide in her favor, yes. Thus, I will be impartial. I will try to be impartial, although I'm not sure that I will always be successful." The same approach was expressed by another judge [26] who stated that "empathy is needed for preparing everything for issuing the just, impartial judgment . . . but in the case of issuing the verdict—at this point, we are driven mostly by the binding laws." This sentiment was echoed by several other judges [10, 11, 24].

In some respects, such a strategy can be seen as a cautious explanation—one that acknowledges the existence of judges' empathy but neutralizes potential criticism by downplaying empathy's significance and role in verdicts. Still, though accepting a premise that empathy does not impact judgment may seem reasonable, questions do arise. Can judges truly regulate their internal thought processes, compartmentalize empathy in early phases, and precisely delineate and control the impact of empathy in their decisions? Perhaps this approach could be refined if judges explicitly differentiated the purpose of empathy during hearings and articulate why it would not interfere with the judgment.

Emphasizing control over empathy

The next strategy employed by judges to reconcile the use of empathy with maintaining impartiality involves setting limits for empathy, on the one hand, and warning of the potential dangers associated with its uncontrolled usage, on the other. Additionally, judges engage in various forms of self-regulation (e.g., distancing, controlling, self-monitoring) to mitigate risks and safeguard impartiality. The underlying idea is that empathy, when properly managed by the judge, does not corrupt the judicial decision-making process. The assumption is that, in general, empathy has its flaws but can be carefully managed by judges.

For example, one justice [8] maintained that there is no equality between being empathic and being partial: "A judge must be aware of the different thought processes going on in his head and notice [them]. Extensive identification with one of the parties can lead to the balance being tilted in favor of that party. We are judges; we can consider, distinguish, and, as I am saying, [in the end] we work by referring to the statutes." This comment refers back to the previous strategy, asserting that empathy can be in use, though before reaching a judgment; here the judge reassured that a decision is determined by law, not empathy, which remains under control. These two arguments complement each other well and, in combination, they appear much more compelling. Nevertheless, this justice also compared judges to chefs, stating that, beyond the ingredients, there is also a need for experience, knowledge, and empathy. This metaphor stresses the role of the personal in judging: That, too, is unavoidable and desirable, but should be subject to some self-monitoring by judges.

In a poignant reflection, a judge [16], while navigating the intricate relationship between empathy and impartiality, inadvertently intertwined empathy with compassion, lamenting that "There are situations in which the circumstances of a given person are so difficult—my heart is simply broken—but I have to decide against her, to her disadvantage. Then, [I have] a huge boxing match with myself, but I cannot allow myself to be partial. . . . This is an issue of ethos." Here, the judge grapples with the emotional toll of difficult cases, acknowledging the internal struggle between empathic impulses (easy empathy) and the imperative of impartial adjudication. In like manner, another judge [23, likewise 13] highlighted the importance of self-monitoring in preserving impartiality:

> But if it would happen during a trial that I begin to tilt too much toward one party . . . then I immediately moderate myself, . . . [I say to myself], "Wait a second, I can't go that route since I must base my findings on facts to reach an objective decision." Yes, I think, that adequately balancing all these ingredients allows me to be an objective judge.

This introspective process of self-correction (see Roach Anleu, Mack 2021: 105–106, 191–192), a kind of work on oneself, is a crucial component of the judicial ethos, ensuring that personal inclinations do not overshadow the objective assessment of facts and legal principles. Quite a different matter is the adequacy of such attempts on the part of a judge.

One judge [32], who possessed a deep understanding of empathy and its role in the judicial realm, provided profound insights into the impact of empathy-based biases and their management during trials. She articulated a conscientious approach toward recognizing and moderating personal biases rooted in her life experiences, emphasizing the importance of maintaining impartiality. This justice commented, "I try to be careful about my feelings which recall my life experiences, [but] can understand such situations. And then I rather tend to think about myself, whether I favor [someone], and then I wonder whether I do not . . . lean toward the other side." This statement underscored her self-awareness and vigilance in ensuring fair treatment of all parties involved. Furthermore, she described how her similar experiences with litigants prompted her to distance herself from identifying too closely with any party. She elaborated on ongoing internal processes during court proceedings—a strong sense of reflexivity sets off alarm bells, signaling potential biases. This reflective capacity allows her (and other judges) to monitor their reactions and regulate their responses (on the importance of reflexivity to regulate empathy see Törnqvist, Wettergren 2023; Missalle 2023). She elucidated, "I can give myself time, which gives me a chance to see the situation. . . . It's not possible to be separated from one's own perspective, but it is possible to detect these moments in which I identify [with someone], 'too much,' when someone's perspective is close to me." This justice's ability to maintain emotional self-awareness and discern her empathetic identification with a party has enabled her to hold empathy at bay in her judicial decision-making.

Another judge [35] outlined her process for managing empathic impulses, illustrating how it contributes to achieving a state closer to objectivity. In an insightful anecdote, this woman openly shared her battle with a specific bias: her strong inclination to protect animal rights. She candidly acknowledged the challenge of navigating cases related to this subject matter, stating, "In such issues, one really needs to have the skills to lock this inside oneself, to prevent it from surfacing, to treat people in just fashion, without imposing one's worldview." This admission not only demonstrates this judge's self-awareness but also sheds light on a delicate balancing act required to ensure a fair decision-making process. As in the previous case, this judge's recognition and control of empathetic impulses are powerful tools in the pursuit of impartiality in her decision-making. However, an important question arises as to if or how she assesses the adequacy of such control: Is this a genuinely rationalized process or a potential area for further scrutiny and refinement? This highlights another challenge in maintaining impartiality in judicial decision-making, particularly when dealing with deeply ingrained personal convictions.

Emphasizing self-monitoring and self-discipline, the pathways of control (a form of easy empathy) unveil different processes of self-management of the effects of empathetic responses. However, this should be supplemented by more data based on courtroom observations of judges, as well as by a more detailed description from judges of how these processes work (for an Australian case, see Mack et al. 2021: 9).

De-absolutizing formal impartiality and prioritizing empathy

An interesting strategy for reconciling empathy with impartiality is a) to avoid absolutizing or fetishizing impartiality when faced with real inequality between the parties in judicial proceedings or, alternatively, b) to understand impartiality in a manner more justice oriented than identical treatment oriented. In the first scenario, impartiality is not necessarily the paramount value, creating room for empathy, while in the second, "just" impartiality may even necessitate empathy. Despite the fact that only two judges ventured into this territory, it is remarkably interesting and deserving of exploration due to the treatment of judicial impartiality as nearly sacrosanct within the judiciary.

A judge [1] representing the first option, while acknowledging the crucial role of impartiality in the judicial process, astutely pointed out that impartiality should not be interpreted as ignoring the incompetence or ineptitude of any party involved. This nuanced perspective recognizes that the pursuit of justice cannot solely rely on strict adherence to formal impartiality when blatant imbalances or deficiencies exist. The judge further explored the complexities of finding a balance between parties, suggesting that in cases where an imbalance is evident, actions may be justified that deviate from the rigid confines of formal impartiality. Similarly, a judge [22] representing the second option emphasized the importance of contextualizing impartiality within the broader framework of justice and fairness. While impartiality remains a fundamental principle of the judicial system, it cannot be divorced from the pursuit of justice and a sense of fairness. The judge argued that rigidly adhering to impartiality—without considering the unique circumstances and needs of distinct cases—actually risks perpetuating injustice. This incisive viewpoint reframes impartiality as a means of achieving justice rather than an end in and of itself—thereby allowing empathy to play a constructive role in promoting equitable outcomes.

The de-absolutizing of formal impartiality is certainly a bold argument. In some sense, the very presenting of such a view was an act of bravery, as it casts doubt on certain professional dogmas and inviolable premises. Although it was mentioned by only two interviewees, this way of thinking has led to a rethinking of the hierarchy of judicial values and principles.

Concluding discussion

The overriding discovery—that judges believe there to be no contradiction between using empathy and maintaining impartiality—should not be underestimated. This is significant, as it reveals a more positive attitude of judges toward empathy than one might expect; this revelation is all the more striking given the profound authority of traditional legal positivism in Poland (see Mańko 2013) and the continued prevalence of the stone-faced ideal.

By way of explaining this disregard for potential conflict in the empathy-impartiality relationship, it could be argued that a general societal preference for empathy has been driving this point of view. Judges may strive to uphold both values or express a belief in their relatively harmonious coexistence, especially considering the importance placed on empathy in social discourse. Frankly, it would seem absurd to argue against empathy. Moreover, the tense atmosphere surrounding the judiciary in Poland during the interviews could have further influenced the judges in our cohort to emphasize the significance of empathy in their decision-making processes; this could, perhaps, counteract the accusations of judicial insensitivity propagated by the government at the time. In the face of such attacks, there may have been a mechanism of self-protection. However, it should be stressed that most judges did not seek to secure an iron-clad image of the judiciary, but rather acknowledged some of its problems as well as instances of unjust judicial behaviors.

The complete absence of voices in our study to back the usual conviction that empathy and impartiality stand in conflict may be surprising, and yet a study conducted among Australian judicial officers revealed parallels. Indeed, several of the Australians "describe[d] their judicial practice as entailing impartiality and empathy, almost as complementary forces requiring careful and persistent monitoring of their boundaries" (Roach Anleu, Mack 2021: 74). However, as mentioned, Polish judges are often hyperactive—frequently playing a dominant role in witness questioning, managing evidence, and selecting court-appointed experts. This hyperactivity (likely shaped by a few factors) may require more empathetic skills of justices in Poland as an offset. The unanimity among judges with respect to an empathy-impartiality compatibility could suggest deeply ingrained tacit beliefs within the judicial community. The prevailing archetypal consensus on the issue—with the research elucidating and articulating these commonly held views—more firmly ingrains the expected, instead of uncovering dissenting opinions.

Nonetheless, the limitations of our research methodology must be acknowledged. In-depth interviews rely heavily on verbal declarations, which may reflect an idealized self-presentation. As such, the outcomes themselves have not been conducive to critical self-reflection, especially considering the formal roles and professional identity of the Polish judges in our sample. Furthermore, the research project did not compare these verbal accounts with actual practices: Such a comparison could provide a more refined understanding of how empathy is expressed verbally and then balanced with impartiality in practice.

One thing of great consequence should be pointed out: Even when judges did not see empathy's potential role in securing impartiality (itself a telling fact), they were largely silent about the positive role of empathy in upholding judicial impartiality (see Lee 2014: 148). Only one judge [9; with judge 19 suggesting linkage] emphasized that empathy "does not disturb impartiality and even strengthens it. Absolutely, it is helpful." However, this exception—even formulated as a general observation, without details—suggests that the potential for empathy to serve as an antidote to biases, prejudices, and closed-mindedness was not a primary consideration for the participants. Even those judges who agreed with the definition of empathy as an overall, open-mindedness seemed not to explore this possibility. Thus, the view that empathy can work as a de-biasing device (Maibom 2022) does not resonate with how these judges perceive the issue.

References

Bandes, Susan A. 1996. "Empathy, Narrative, and Victim Impact Statements." *University of Chicago Law Review* 63: 361–412.

Bandes, Susan A. 2017. "Compassion and the Rule of Law." *International Journal of Law in Context* 13(2): 184–196.

Bergman Blix, Stina and Åsa Wettergren. 2016. "Empathy and Objectivity in the Legal Process: The Case of Swedish Prosecutors." *Journal of Scandinavian Studies in Criminology and Crime Prevention* 17: 19–35.

Colby, Thomas B. 2012. "In Defense of Judicial Empathy." *Minnesota Law Review* 96: 1945–2015.

Fissell, Brenner. 2016. "Modern Critiques of Judicial Empathy: A Revised Intellectual History." *Michigan State Law Review* 817: 817–851.

Franks, Mary A. 2011. "*Lies, Damned Lies, and Judicial Empathy.*" *Washburn Law Journal* 51(1): 61–72.

Lee, Rebecca K. 2014. "Judging Judges: Empathy as the Litmus Test for Impartiality." *University of Cincinnati Law Review* 82: 145–206.

Mack, Kathy and Sheryn Roach Anleu. 2010. "Performing Impartiality: Judicial Demeanour and Legitimacy." *Law & Social Inquiry* 35(1): 137–173.

Mack, Kathy et al. 2021. "Judicial Impartiality, Bias and Emotion." *Australian Journal of Administrative Law* 28(2): 66–82.

Maibom, Heidi L. 2022. *The Space between*. Oxford: Oxford University Press.

Mańko, Rafał. 2013. "Weeds in the Gardens of Justice? The Survival of Hyperpositivism in Polish Legal Culture as a Symptom/Sinthome." *Pólemos* 7(2): 207–233. https://doi.org/10.1515/pol-2013-0011

Maroney, Terry A. 2011. "The Persistent Cultural Script of Judicial Dispassion." *California Law Review* 99: 629–681.

Maroney, Terry and Phillip Ackerman-Lieberman. 2014. "As a Father Shows Compassion for His Children." *Journal of Law, Religion and State* 2(3): 240–275.

Missalle, Alessandra. 2023. *Emotions in Legal Decisions: The Construction of Objective Narratives in Italian Criminal Trials*. Uppsala: Uppsala University Press.

Roach Anleu, Sharyn and Kathy Mack. 2017. *Performing Judicial Authority in the Lower Courts*. London: Palgrave Macmillan.

Roach Anleu, Sharyn and Kathy Mack. 2021. *Judging and Emotion A Socio-Legal Analysis*. London: Routledge.

Shaman, Jeffrey M. 1996. "The Impartial Judge: Detachment or Passion?" *DePaul Law Review* 45: 605–632.

Törnqvist, Nina and Åsa Wettergren. 2023. "Epistemic Emotions in Prosecutorial Decision Making." *Journal of Law and Society* 50: 208–230. https://doi.org/10.1111/jols.12421

West, Robin. 2011. "The Anti-Empathic Turn." *Georgetown Law Faculty Publications and Other Works* 678: 1–57.

Wojciechowski, Maciej et al. 2015. "Emotional Labour of Judges." *Archiwum Filozofii Prawa i Filozofii Społecznej* 1(10): 97–110.

Zipursky, Benjamin. 2012. "Anti-Empathy and Dispassionateness in Adjudication." In *Passions and Emotions: NOMOS LIII*, edited by James E. Fleming. 304–314. New York: NYU Press.

6 Developing judicial empathy through training methods

A psychological perspective

Ewa Wilczek-Rużyczka

Introduction

Empathy has been a topic addressed by scholars across numerous academic fields. Increasingly, it is becoming an element bridging interdisciplinary researchers investigating its essence, the way it functions, and how it can be harnessed. The literature highlights the importance of empathy in various professional niches, such as in the medical and psychological fields or other professions holding public trust. In Anglo-Saxon discourse, there is also a perceptible discussion about the significance of empathy in the legal professions, particularly among judges.

The origin of empathy and its determinants

Empathy, according to some authors, is simply the ability to resonate with the emotions of another person, to understand what they are experiencing, and to feel what they feel. This ability is of immense value when striving to understand as well as to provide help and support to another person, because an empathetic individual is characterized by care, openness, and extraordinary sensitivity. An empathetic person is also capable of attentive listening, focusing on both the verbal and nonverbal communication of the speaker. Empathy enables perception of what another person is feeling, even if that person does not or cannot directly articulate this aloud (Orloff 2020).

More significantly, an increasing number of scholars are currently looking at empathy more broadly and holistically, recognizing it as not only the ability to perceive another's emotional state but also to grasp and convey that rapport. The ability to empathize with and comprehend the experiences and feelings of others is an invaluable and helpful skill that facilitates everyday social functioning. Thus, empathy is one of the crucial social competencies, which, although not truly innate, can be developed through appropriate exercises and training, as confirmed by numerous studies.

This is vital because low empathetic skills—or their absence—can lead to many negative consequences. These include, among others, the potential for antisocial and aggressive behavior, as well as the impeding of interpersonal

DOI: 10.4324/9781003546580-7

relationships. Auspiciously, the development of empathy is possible not only in early childhood but even in adulthood; this competency can be enhanced and refined, be it through psychoeducation provided by psychologists and psychotherapists, acquisition of knowledge about empathy, or participation in empathy training sessions (Wilczek-Rużyczka 2017). For example, research results have demonstrated the benefits of developing empathy among medical professionals (Wilczek-Rużyczka 2017), as well as students, including law students (Wilczek-Rużyczka 2024). Training in this skillset should be a particularly valued component of the curricula for future as well as current professionals working in healthcare, social assistance, and the legal fields—in other words, persons whose vocation involves support for individuals facing life challenges (Salazar et al. 2023).

In recent years, the social sciences have made significant progress in discovering the mechanisms that allow a person to feel what another feels. Consistent evidence suggests that empathizing with the emotions of others is associated with activation of neural structures that also operate during one's own experiences of those emotions. Some of the neural activation shared between personal and extra-personal experiences seems to be automatically triggered. However, recent research also indicates that empathy is a highly flexible phenomenon, with responses that are influenced by various factors—such as contextual evaluation, the interpersonal relationship between the empathizer and others, or the viewpoint from which another person is observed. Therefore, empathy is the ability to understand, resonate with, and identify with the emotions, feelings, and perspectives of others. The capacity to empathize with others' experiences, understand their needs, and respond to them with empathy and understanding plays a crucial role in interpersonal relationships, social bonding, and helping others in difficult situations (Singer, Lamm 2009: 81–96).

Empathy is thus an important communication skill encompassing three dimensions: the emotional, cognitive, and behavioral. It has been proven that a high level of empathy among healthcare and social service workers means more effective fulfillment of their occupational roles. In the company of specialists who exhibit empathy, others sense a safe space in which their thoughts and problems can be freely expressed. Although the importance of empathy is undeniable, a significant percentage of these professionals seem to struggle with adopting an empathetic communication model in daily practice. Factors that negatively affect the development of empathy include a high caseload, lack of adequate time, a narrow task-oriented focus, and a lack of education in empathy. Developing this toolset should not only be a primary goal in the education of students in health and social work but also a subject area in continuing education and professional development for practitioners (Moudatsou et al. 2020). Unsurprisingly, all this pertains to legal professionals, too—including, above all, judges.

This description evidences, among other things, that empathy plays a key part in relationships and interactions. However, for more effective interpersonal communication to be achieved, certain conditions conducive to empathetic behavior must be met—both at the individual and institutional levels. The key determinants can be classified as follows (Wilczek-Rużyczka 2008):

1. Ontogenetic development: Empathy is often considered an emotion that changes throughout a person's development. Research suggests that empathetic reactions appear as early as infancy, which may indicate the existence of an innate mechanism, though this is not conclusively proven. The development of empathy occurs alongside social experiences and the process of socialization.
2. Personal factors: An individual's personality, temperament, abilities, and gender influence the level of empathy. Research suggests that females often exhibit higher levels than males.
3. Family conditions: The family structure, parenting style, and quality of family relationships can affect the development of empathy in children. Children raised in large families may exhibit higher levels of empathy than only children. Families where emotional needs are met and emotional security prevails can contribute to the growth of empathy in children.
4. Moral values: The level of empathy may depend on an individual's moral development and level of religiosity.
5. Living conditions: Living conditions, such as urbanization, life pace, and exposure to various situations, can influence the level of empathy. Intense stimulation may lead to a weakening of empathetic reactivity.
6. Sensitivity to suffering: The ability to empathize may also be related to the level of sensitivity to the suffering of others. Individuals with higher emotional sensitivity may be more inclined to respond empathetically to the needs of others.
7. Professional orientation: Career choice can influence the level of empathy. People who choose professions related to social services or medicine often exhibit higher empathy.
8. Characteristics of the object and situation: The intensity of empathetic reactions depends on the characteristics of the receiver of empathy, such as psychological and emotional closeness between granter and receiver and the emotional expression of the latter. A situation in which the receiver is in a distressing position may evoke a stronger empathetic reaction than a pleasant one.
9. Situation clarity: Situations where the causes of suffering, distress, or discomfort are clear and explicit may foster empathetic responses.

In summary, empathy is a complex skill shaped by many factors, including the personal, family, professional, and social. Its determinants can be diverse, stemming from both biological and social as well as environmental factors. Empathy develops alongside life experiences and the socialization process, but is also influenced by individual personality traits, career choices, and situations.

The importance of empathy in interpersonal and professional relationships

In recent years, numerous behavioral, cognitive, and functional imaging studies have demonstrated that individuals understand the emotional and affective states expressed by others through a neural structure that generates such states within the empathizer. This mechanism leads to shared representations, which form one significant aspect of empathy, though not the only one. It is suggested that other components—such as an individual's ability to monitor and regulate cognitive and emotional responses to avoid interpersonal tensions or conflict—are equally essential in a functional model of empathy. One serviceable model assumes that empathy relies on distinct mechanisms for processing information; on that basis, it predicts various structural or functional dysfunctions depending on which mechanism is disrupted (Decety, Jackson 2006: 54–58).

Thus, empathy plays a crucial role in both interpersonal and professional relationships. The importance of empathy stems from its impact on the quality of communication, understanding, and support in human interactions. In interpersonal relationships, empathy allows for understanding the emotions, feelings, and experiences of another person, which leads to a higher level of acceptance and respect in the relationship.

Demonstrating empathy enables the formation of deeper emotional bonds with others, which, consequently, strengthens relationships and brings people closer together. Additionally, empathetic responses to others' difficulties and problems help them feel seen and heard, which can bring relief and a sense of support. For example, in the medical profession, the first researcher who considered empathy as one of the most important components of the relationship between caregiver and patient was Carl Rogers. He confirmed that empathy is a factor that increases therapeutic effectiveness. In Rogers' definition, empathy is the accurate understanding of another person's internal experience, which aligns with Charles Truax's classic, broader definition of empathy, describing it as the accurate perception of a client's current feelings and the tuning of verbal communication to convey this understanding to the client. Based on this definition, many researchers have argued that empathy is both a skill and an attitude. In this context, empathy is the ability to communicate one's understanding of another person's feelings as well as the causes of those feelings. In the context of professional relationships among employees, empathy in the workplace facilitates effective communication, understanding the needs of team members, and collaboration in problem-solving.

An important aspect of empathy is also its role in conflict resolution. Demonstrating empathy opens a window through which to look at the world from another's perspective, leading to better understanding and compromise; empathy contributes to higher-quality relationships, strengthens trust, and improves communication and collaboration. This is achieved through skillful listening to the other side, expressing understanding, and seeking common solutions. Since this helps avoid misunderstandings and antagonisms, conflicts can be more effectively resolved through dialogue. This also applies to individuals in legal professions—such as those representing conflicting parties—and, in the case of judges, it allows for a deeper understanding of trial participants and their choices.

Methods of measuring empathy

Initial thoughts

To measure the level of empathy between professionals and laypeople and to identify the need for empathy training as well as its direct effects, precise tools for empathy measurement are necessary. The challenge in this regard stems from the fact that, despite agreement among researchers on the importance of empathy as a human trait, there has been a long-standing disagreement regarding its formal definition. The divergence of opinions concerns the nature of empathy—whether it involves sharing another person's emotions or the ability and willingness to mentally place oneself in another person's situation. In other words, the debate revolves around whether empathy is linked to emotional processes or cognitive processes. It is difficult to develop an effective measurement tool when no consensus exists regarding the definition of the phenomenon being measured.

Researchers generally agree that empathy is a multidimensional concept. Therefore, when measuring its level and analyzing results, it is important to understand which aspect of empathy a particular tool measures. To gain a more comprehensive picture of empathy levels, it is advisable to use more than one measurement method whenever possible.

One analysis of existing methods for measuring empathy among adults relies upon three different approaches. The first involves self-assessment based on a standardized questionnaire filled out by the individual whose empathy is being measured. The second approach evaluates empathy through a questionnaire completed by someone who had experienced empathy, such as, for example, a party in a legal proceeding assessing the empathetic behavior of the defense attorney, the prosecutor, and/or the judge. The third approach is based on an assessment of empathy by an outside observer, either through a standardized questionnaire or according to specific criteria. The choice of approach depends on the situation and the goal of the measurement. The first approach allows for large-scale studies for selection or comparison purposes, while the second and third approaches can help assess and improve empathy in medical, social, and legal professions.

Joanne M. Hemmerdinger et al. (2007)—in a review article on empathy tests used in medical field studies—compiled 36 tests, of which 6 were based on self-assessment, 5 on patient assessments of the doctor or nurse, and 17 on observer assessments. Methods for measuring empathy in adults can mostly be applied or adapted for use in other contexts, if their psychometric properties have been empirically verified.

Self-assessment methods for measuring empathy

Most commonly used methods for measuring empathy are based on self-assessment, including widely used scales and questionnaires, such as the Emotional Empathy Tendency Questionnaire (Mehrabian, Epstein 1972), the Interpersonal Reactivity Index (Davis 1983), two versions of the Jefferson Scale (Hojat et al. 2003, 2002a, 2002b), the Empathy Quotient Scale (Baron-Cohen, Wheelwright 2004), and the Emotional-Cognitive Empathy Questionnaire EEP (Wilczek-Rużyczka 2024). These scales assume that adults possess self-awareness and the ability to assess and express opinions about their own attitudes and behaviors. However, as found in our study of a cohort of judges, there is a risk with most personality tests in that respondents a) lack the necessary self-awareness and ability to articulate opinions about their own attitudes and b) may provide socially desirable answers, leading to inaccurate results. Therefore, it is recommended that data obtained be corroborated through one method with findings from another measurement tool.

Measurement of empathy based on the assessment of the person experiencing it

Measuring empathetic behaviors based on the assessment of the receiving individual, such as a medical patient or trial participant, is much less commonly used. The number of available and well-validated psychometric tools for this purpose is limited compared to self-assessment methods. Some of the first questionnaires were designed to measure patients' perceptions of their therapists' behaviors, such as the Relationship Questionnaire by Charles Truax and Robert Carkhuff (1967) and the Relationship Inventory by Godfrey Barrett-Lennard (1986), both of which include a separate empathy scale.

Observer-based assessment of empathy using standardized questionnaires or specific criteria

This group of tools includes the projective method, intentionally selected for description by the examined person, whose descriptions are then evaluated by a competent and independent evaluator. This allows for the assessment of emotional, cognitive, and behavioral components of empathy employing precisely the projective method (Wilczek-Rużyczka 2002).

Developing empathy through training

The primary goal of training is to develop essential skills for both interpersonal relationships and self-management. Various forms of group training in interpersonal skills have been implemented in Poland for students as well as professionals in psychology, medicine, pedagogy, and management; such training has yet to be implemented among students and professionals in the field of law. The objectives of the training have been articulated in various ways, all focusing on optimizing practical psychological skills crucial to human interactions—such as respect, authenticity, specificity, initiative, directness, openness, emotional engagement, courage in confronting differing viewpoints, self-awareness, and, most importantly here, empathy.

Particularly valuable is the practice of discussing one's subjective feelings and perceptions related to current group dynamics, avoiding generalizations and theoretical discussions, addressing individuals directly, and spontaneously expressing one's thoughts and feelings. Given the low levels of empathy identified in this group, previous successes, especially the outcomes of empathy training, support the extension of such training to law students (Wilczek-Rużyczka 2024), as well as to various legal professionals, including justices in lower courts. Indeed, the judges participating in our in-depth interviews concurred that there is a necessity for and value in such training. Our interviewees, experienced judges, recognized the importance of empathy in the execution of their professional duties and advocated for the implementation of training even at the student level. Selected statements from the interview transcripts illustrate this point well:

- "I believe that judges should be trained in soft skills. They should at least have the opportunity to view their profession not only as issuing legal judgments, but also as fulfilling a role that involves understanding people. Therefore, empathy training could be beneficial."
- "In terms of empathy, judges should certainly be trained in this area. This training, prior to entering the profession, should also cover soft skills through unconventional activities, such as visits to social welfare centers or correctional facilities to observe the impact of judicial decisions."
- "In general, I think it's very valuable for judges to be trained in all soft skills. I believe that the way we are perceived by society, which is often negative, might be due to a lack of communication skills and other soft skills."
- "I think it's very necessary. Workshops with small groups in a supportive environment would be the way to go."

The feedback from the judges in our sample—both the unquoted and those quoted earlier—suggests a clear need for developing empathy and stress management skills. This is particularly key in the challenging environment of the Polish judicial system, which is stressful for the judges themselves, requiring decision-making under the pressure of deadlines and with a high volume of cases. The judges with whom we spoke emphasized a need for greater sensitivity and understanding, not only toward defendants, witnesses, and other anxious individuals who may be appearing in court for the first time but also toward their judicial peers.

Therefore, it is essential to implement empathy training based on well-prepared programs that consider both the guiding principles and the specific nature of a judge's work. When preparing and implementing such training, the following elements and recommendations should be considered (Paulus, Meinken 2022):

- Training methods: Role-playing, discussions, feedback sessions, lectures, individual and group work, conversations with experts, and observation of example interactions
- Training content: Communication challenges (theory and a conversation guide), self-reflection, learning from personal experiences, the theory and significance of empathy, perspective-taking, learning from others' experiences, and empathetic behaviors

Given that a significant part of empathy involves cognitive processing—a conscious process that entails a decision regarding whether to engage at all—it is also important to consider whether this choice might be hindered by factors such as:

- Biologically dysfunctional brain processing
- Social learning to ignore certain feelings or thoughts
- Stress from environmental factors, preventing people from seeing beyond their situation
- Subconscious brain processing, e.g., a fear that paralyzes cognitive processing
- Empathy linked to familiarity: weak empathy may be associated with a lack of connection to those who are culturally similar (Segal et al. 2017)

Stephen Bennett, too, has pointed out other limitations in exercising empathy that may reduce the effectiveness of empathy training, including:

- Lack of time
- Lack of energy
- Fear (Segal et al. 2017)

These considerations are particularly relevant for judges, who often face a large number of exacting cases over extended periods of time. In the execution of their work, it is also important to address:

- Burnout and dehumanization, which can also limit empathy
- Barriers resulting from education
- Lack of empathetic communication skills
- The organization and management of judicial work
- Time pressures
- Misconceptions about empathy, such as the belief that it is unnecessary or time-consuming
- Empathy seen as disrupting objectivity
- Overlooking emotional problems

- Stress and stress management
- Personality traits, such as narcissism (Segal et al. 2017)

Obstacles to the expression of empathy are rooted in various factors and are often a result of education, work organization, individual opinions and beliefs, and misunderstandings of empathetic communication. With reference to the interviews we conducted, the judges in our sample also pointed out specific challenges, drawn from their professional experiences, that hamper the expression of empathy:

- Witness barriers: "People often can't articulate their thoughts."
- Lack of time to reflect upon a case: "The workload is so heavy that the practical functioning of empathy suffers, because there isn't even time to consider what the case involves."
- Lack of interpersonal skills and personality issues: "It seems that it's not due to a lack of substantive knowledge, but a lack of interpersonal skills. I don't want to say emotional intelligence, but there's some of that."
- Physical and organizational barriers: "I can imagine that, for some, seeing a judge in robes with a chain [of office] might be intimidating and create a barrier to communication."
- Formal language: "The barrier of legal jargon often kills the message, making it incomprehensible to the parties."
- Routine: "Falling into routine is detrimental as it leads to a loss of empathy, because we apply predetermined mechanisms to situations that are similar."
- Personal well-being and the home situation: "External factors, like feeling unwell, can impact decision-making as we are only human."
- Previous experiences: "Experiences in private and professional life, especially those where empathetic decisions have led to disappointment, can hinder empathy."

These statements suggest that hindrances to a judge's empathy can be both individual and structural-organizational. While the former can be overcome to some extent individually, the latter requires the involvement of superiors and changes in the organization of court work.

The assumptions of the original empathy training

Empathy training is a method based on experiential learning, achieved through participation in small group meetings (6–12 people). In this method, both the content and the learning process are unique. The latter is supplemented by observation and experiencing the behaviors of others. The focus of learning is self-awareness, sensitivity, empathy toward others, perceiving and verbalizing one's own feelings as well as the feelings of others, and the ability to communicate such emotions. This is especially important when using this method in the training of professionals in fields whose focus is on helping others—this means not only social workers but also lawyers and justices.

These professionals, often under the pressure of deadlines, are forced to concentrate mainly on following procedures, reducing their contact with individuals (who are often in posttraumatic or stressful situations) to a schematic interrogation. Information obtained in this manner often fails to deepen an understanding of the problem or fails to contribute to just decisions. Therefore, empathy training aims to create circumstances that facilitate the acquisition of experiences and skills that increase self-confidence, improve emotional understanding and control in vexing situations, enhance awareness of personal responsibility in relationships with those in need, and, finally, optimize communication skills. The starting point here is the belief that the primary tool in this regard is the helping person or the legal arbitrator—a thinking, feeling individual with specific knowledge but oriented toward assisting others in their difficulties. Procedural elements, although necessary, are secondary and should be applied in specific cases. Thus, the goal of empathy training is to help in understanding oneself and others (in relation to their dependent function) and to enhance those qualities that, from a psychological perspective, relate to the basic spheres of human functioning—emotional, cognitive, and behavioral.

In the emotional sphere, this training aims to:

1. Awaken sensitivity and an openness to others
2. Develop the ability to empathize with another person's situation
3. Build emotional connections with others
4. Stimulate motivation to act on behalf of others

In the cognitive sphere, this training aims to:

1. Convey knowledge about feelings expressed in both verbal and nonverbal communication
2. Raise awareness of another person's difficult situation
3. Teach the perception and verbalization of feelings in oneself and others
4. Understand another person's perspective

In the behavioral sphere, it aims to:

1. Initiate contact
2. Engage in nonverbal and verbal communication
3. Communicate in a concrete, authentic, and nonjudgmental manner
4. Learn prosocial behaviors

It is important to emphasize that the purpose and method of the training will be made known to participants prior to commencement of the sessions. Group activities (guided by consecutive tasks) will provide the material for addressing the issues outlined in the training objectives. The most commonly used methods will include modeling, simulated scenes in pairs, various psychodrama techniques, imaginative situations, visualization, and music (e.g., Ennio Morricone). Each thematic exercise will be followed by a discussion on the purpose and practical usefulness of the applied method. The training sessions will conclude with a discussion of the theoretical foundations of the methods and techniques used and any issues arising from the training conducted.

Original empathy training program

The fundamental assumption of empathy training is that it will develop a sensitivity toward others, the perception and verbalization of feelings in oneself and others, and the ability to understand and communicate with other individuals. A goal of empathy training is to enhance traits that, from a psychological perspective, relate to the basic spheres of human functioning—the emotional, cognitive, and behavioral. The trainer's role is to create an atmosphere of trust, kindness, and safety in a milieu in which members of the group (6–12 people) can experience their behaviors and reactions to others' behaviors.

The training duration entails three sessions of six hours each, during which the following content is planned:

1. Imparting knowledge about feelings and communication (both verbal and nonverbal), considering empathy and its significance in communication and helping
2. Ensuring participants have pleasant experiences and receive feedback about themselves, as well as relaxation; listening to selected pieces of Morricone's music, while the group undergoes a visual induction using the colors of the rainbow, closing with a discussion
3. Exercising openness; using psycho-drawing, and the theme of "my door," closing with a discussion
4. Exercising acceptance; gaining acceptance in the group, nonverbal expression of acceptance in the group, closing with a discussion
5. Practicing listening with understanding; exercise in three-person groups, closing with a discussion
6. Exercising nonverbal expressions of emotions; using nonverbal signals to show warmth and other feelings in the group, closing with a discussion
7. Practicing, experiencing, and sharing another person's psychological state and recognizing the same feelings; listening to Morricone's music and empathizing with another person's psychological state, exercise in pairs, closing with a discussion
8. A training participant's presentation of a difficult relationship with a client, closing with a discussion
9. Practicing (in pairs) the assessment of received signals of others' feelings, making a list of skills
10. Practicing formulation of an appropriate, sympathetic response (in threes)

11. Practicing delivery of an understanding response (in threes)
12. Exercising giving and receiving in the group, closing with a discussion
13. Two-person discussion groups; how would you act if you were to help your closest companion?

The following tips can be used to assist in achievement of the goals:

1. Put yourself in the other person's situation.
2. Stay with them in the same place and time.
3. Ask yourself the question they asked you.
4. Try to experience the same feelings that the person is likely experiencing.
5. Tell them what you would like to hear in that situation.
6. Do unto others as you would have them do unto you.

Expected outcomes of the original empathy training for judges

The final effects of the proposed empathy training can be considered from different perspectives. The focus is on results related to the optimization of the individual's prosocial functioning, their internal changes, self-awareness, and self-development. Empathy training induces beneficial transformations in sensitivity toward others. During a training session, feedback is usually provided, increasing the ability of participants to understand and predict what the receiver of empathy is experiencing and how that person is perceived. Addressed, too, are actions and reactions evoked in specific settings. Although research results in this area are not uniform, many studies have indeed noted an increase in empathy as an outcome of empathy training (see Wu et al. 2024: 1250).

Early research conducted by Elaine La Monica et al. (1976: 447) indicates that empathy training increases awareness of one's own emotions and transforms motivation toward greater responsibility for one's development. Self-esteem is also higher after training sessions than before, and its effects persist in everyday life and one's professional career. Empathy training also amends the level of openness toward oneself and others, increases self-acceptance and self-worth, and reduces a tendency to control others. Such training also alters the perception of others, leading to better understanding and a favorable view of their behavioral traits. It also brings about changes in interpersonal functioning and communication skills. Therefore, empathy training should improve individual functioning, render a person more open to new information and experiences, and reduce inflexibility.

This is particularly relevant because, according to Zebeda Sherif et al. (2018), communication requires extensive knowledge of empathy and empathic skills. Sherif and his colleagues argued that developing empathy knowledge, as well as training it, has an impact on attitudes, competencies, and behavior. In turn, competencies affect empathic and communication skills, while behavior supports the ability to acquire qualifications.

Taking into consideration findings drawn from the body of research conducted heretofore, it is logically expected that a program of empathy training tailored to judges in Poland will yield similar results as those achieved elsewhere. Participants may be dealing with distinct psychological issues, but it is likely that emotions will arise that will bring them closer to their peers in the training session cohort; participants undergo an encounter characterized by a detachment from the usual social roles and conventions and accompanied by an experience of harmony and unity with others. The training group itself contributes to a deepening of the participants' self-awareness and self-control; this increases their sensitivity to others' experiences and needs, their ability to recognize feelings in themselves and others, and verbal and nonverbal communication, which is so essential for an empathetic judge. The meaningful outcomes of earlier training sessions—at different periods of time, in different countries, and regardless of a given cohort's idiosyncrasies—have manifested in personalized relationships and self-empowerment, leading to closer emotional relationships and increased self-confidence among participants.

Summary

Recent studies have shown that legal professionals, including judges, are more susceptible to symptoms of stress, anxiety, depression, and burnout than other professional groups and the general population. These symptoms are associated, among other things, with low levels of empathy. Bearing in mind that empathy is an inescapable element in legal practice, it can—especially during client interactions, in stressful conditions, and when encircled by an unsupportive work milieu—ameliorate the emotional distress and burnout that can, ultimately, affect lawyer-client interactions negatively (Chlap, Brown 2022).

Thus, the ability to engage in interpersonal reciprocity, which requires a high level of empathy, is not only psychologically and therapeutically valuable, but it is also identified with a moral obligation, rendering empathy a criterion for professionalism. There is potential to enhance the quality of interpersonal relationships effectively and with dependable results. Among other means, this can be achieved through training methods that build empathy. This is not only an emotional reaction but, above all, a valued competency in many professions. Moreover, empathy is no longer relegated to the typical helping professions such as nursing, teaching, and social work but also pertains to judges: It impacts the intensity of focus on patients, social services delivery, legal assistance, and even judicial decision-making. This underscores a consciousness of the fact that, to give effectively, one must also be capable of receiving help (just as much an art as providing it).

It is essential for the judiciary to be prepared to fulfill its responsibilities empathetically. Equally important is judges' awareness of the suffering or difficult life situations faced by those encountered at work. After all, the fate of many an individual depends not only on a judge's professionalism but also on his or her understanding and expression of empathy. Numerous studies confirm that empathetic individuals tend to be more psychologically supportive of those who are suffering and seeking assistance; the empathetic judge is also significantly less inclined to offer superficial reassurances or treat individuals as mere pawns. Empathy also helps prevent dehumanizing behavior. A high level of empathy is therefore not only of psychological and therapeutic value but also a moral obligation that becomes part and parcel of judicial professionalism. Moreover, the enhancement of empathy through training methods constitutes a relatively effective inoculation against the syndrome of professional burnout.

In a narrative review analyzing empathy training studies for social work professionals over the past 30 years, Tony Chiu Ming Lam et al. (2011) addressed the question, "How have people been trained in empathy, and what are the results?" He and his team found that nearly all studies (93%) illustrated positive training results, primarily regarding the development of empathy's cognitive facet (86%). Unfortunately, they did not obtain precise information about the training's impact on the feelings of participants toward one another or their ability and willingness to adopt another person's perspective. The authors advocated for further research that would incorporate the conclusions and suggestions from Lam et al.'s review into the methodology planning. Subsequent meta-analyses by other researchers regarding published results from 18 similar studies (Teding van Berkhout, Malouff 2016) and 15 more recent studies (Paulus, Meinken 2022) have also demonstrated that empathy training can be effective. That evidence suffices to justify the implementation of empathy training in general. However, no significant moderators were found, meaning that neither the session content nor the methods used in the training session influenced the magnitude of the results. To achieve more significant findings in the future, a comparison of various training components is required. It should also be investigated whether empathy training spread over a longer period is more effective and the empathy more sustainable than after single-session training. Naturally, the results of these studies have not only generated answers but also raised new questions. All of this will inspire further training sessions as well as, very importantly, further analyses encompassing other socially significant professional groups—in Poland and the world—where the constructive impact of empathy substantiates the implementation of empathy training.

Conclusions

Regarding legal professionals—particularly judges—it can be stated that:

1. Empathetic listening skills are valuable for practicing judges in the establishment of professional relationships, which are crucial for effective communication. In turn, that state of affairs accelerates the substantive development of cases, enhances professional effectiveness, and can lead to the overall

improvement of the public image of a profession—such as the judiciary in Poland.

2. The use of empathetic communication shortens the time required to establish relationships, which is especially important in lengthy, complex cases.
3. The empathy training proposed in this chapter can teach empathetic communication skills. The effectiveness of developing such a skillset can be evidenced by the outcomes of a legal education program implemented in 1979 at the University of Hawaii School of Law (Barkai, Fine 1983): The benefits gained from empathy training render such programs a valuable complement in legal education.
4. Therefore, and finally, it is recommended that empathy training be implemented not only among individuals in legal professions but also while these individuals are studying law and preparing themselves for a career in the judiciary. Comparative research findings have shown that law students exhibit lower levels of empathy than their peers in psychology and medicine (Wilczek-Rużyczka, Kupczyk 2021). Conversing with and listening to the Polish judges who agreed to participate in our research project, we heard a need for empathy training voiced clearly.

References

Barkai, John L. and Virginia O. Fine. 1983. "Empathy Training for Lawyers and Law Students." *Southwestern University Law Review* 13: 505–529.

Baron-Cohen, Simon and Sally Wheelwright. 2004. "The Empathy Quotient: An Investigation of Adults with Asperger Syndrome or High Functioning Autism, and Normal Sex Differences." *Journal of Autism and Developmental Disorders* 2(34): 163–175.

Barrett-Lennard, Godfrey T. 1986. "The Relationship Inventory Now: Issues and Advances in Theory, Method and Uses." In *The Psychotherapeutic Process*, edited by Leslie S. Greenberg and William M. Pinsof. 439–476. New York: Guilford Press.

Chlap, Nora and Rhonda Brown. 2022. "Relationships between Workplace Characteristics, Psychological Stress, Affective Distress, Burnout and Empathy in Lawyers." *International Journal of the Legal Profession* 29(9): 1–22.

Davis, Mark H. 1983. "The Effects of Dispositional Empathy on Emotional Reactions and Helping: A. Multidimensional Approach." *Journal of Personality and Social Psychology* 51: 167–184.

Decety, Jean and Philip L. Jackson. 2006. "A Social-Neuroscience Perspective on Empathy." *Current Directions in Psychological Science* 15(2): 54–58.

Hemmerdinger, Joanne M. et al. 2007. "A Systematic Review of Tests of Empathy in Medicine." *BMC Medical Education* 7: 24.

Hojat, Mohammadreza et al. 2002a. "Empathy in Medical Students as Related to Academic Performance, Clinical Competence and Gender." *Medical Education* 36: 522–527.

Hojat, Mohammadreza et al. 2002b. "The Jefferson Scale of Physician Empathy: Further Psychometric Data and Differences by Gender and Specialty at Item Level." *Academic Medicine* 77: 58–60.

Hojat, Mohammadreza et al. 2003. "Physician Empathy in Medical Education and Practice: Experience with Jefferson Scale of Physician Empathy." *Seminars in Integrative Medicine* 1: 25–41.

Lam, Tony C. M. et al. 2011. "Empathy Training: Methods, Evaluation Practices, and Validity." *Journal of Multidisciplinary Evaluation* 7(16): 162–200.

La Monica, Elaine L. et al. 1976. "Empathy Training as the Major Thrust of a Staff Development Programme." *Nursing Research* 6(25): 447–451.

Mehrabian, Albert and Norman Epstein. 1972. "A Measure of Emotional Empathy." *Journal of Personality* 4: 525–545.

Moudatsou, Maria et al. 2020. "The Role of Empathy in Health and Social Care Professionals." *Healthcare (Basel)* 8(1): 26.

Orloff, Judith. 2020. *Empatia. Poradnik dla wrażliwych.* Łódź: Feeria.

Paulus, Christoph M. and Saskie Meinken. 2022. "The Effectiveness of Empathy Training in Health Care: A Meta-Analysis of Training Content and Methods." *International Journal of Medical Education* 13: 1–9.

Salazar, Krista et al. 2023. "Our Patients Need Empathy Training Across Healthcare Professions." *American Journal of Pharmaceutical Education* 87(5): 100011.

Segal, Elizabeth A. et al. 2017. *Assessing Empathy.* New York: Columbia University Press.

Sherif, Zebeda A. G. et al. 2018. "Evaluate the Effect of Empathy-Based Training Program on Psychiatric Nurses' Communication Skills." *Journal of Nursing and Health Science* 7(3): 32–41.

Singer, Tania and Claus Lamm. 2009. "The Social Neuroscience of Empathy." *Annals of the New York Academy of Sciences* 1156(1): 81–96.

Teding van Berkhout, Emily and John M. Malouff. 2016. "The Efficacy of Empathy Training: A Meta-Analysis of Randomized Controlled Trials." *Journal of Counseling Psychology.* Jan, 63(1): 32–41.

Truax, Charles B. and Robert F. Carkhuff 1967. *Toward Effective Counseling and Psychotherapy: Training and Practice.* Chicago: Aldine.

Wilczek-Rużyczka, Ewa. 2002. *Empatia i jej rozwój u osób pomagających.* Kraków: Wydawnictwo UJ.

Wilczek-Rużyczka, Ewa. 2008. *Wypalenie zawodowe a empatia u lekarzy i pielęgniarek.* Kraków: Wydawnictwo UJ.

Wilczek-Rużyczka, Ewa. 2017. *Empatia pracowników medycznych.* Warszawa: ABC a Wolters Kluwer business.

Wilczek-Rużyczka, Ewa. 2024. "Empathy as a Determinant of Perceived Stress and Styles of Coping with Stress in Medical, Law and Psychology Students." *Acta Neuropsychologica* 22(2): 151–167.

Wilczek-Rużyczka, Ewa and Michał Kupczyk. 2021. "Level of Empathy and Severity of Psychopathic Traits in Medical, Law and Psychology Students." *Acta Neuropsychologica* 19(4): 411–426.

Wu, Xiao et al. 2024. "Categories of Training to Improve Empathy: A Systematic Review and Meta-Analysis." *Psychological Bulletin* 150: 1237–1260.

Conclusion

Mateusz Stępień

This volume—filling a gap in the law and emotions literature as well as meeting a need for empathy research in the judicial context—opened by highlighting a skill-based approach to reforming and strengthening the judiciary. The effective functioning of this branch of government is dependent on fostering worthy qualities and competencies among judges. The approach we took is rooted deeply in a processual perspective that promotes the training, refining, and integration of unique skills indispensable to the professional role of a justice. Nowhere is this more necessary than in a post-communist country (Poland) that has recently suffered an eight-year (2015–2023) episode of democratic backsliding which explicitly targeted the judiciary. That notwithstanding, the outcomes of our research, observations, and analyses have a bearing on challenges—particularly those surrounding empathy—faced by judges around the world.

Setting aside the possibilities and problems in defining the term, empathy as presented herein is conceptualized as a general ability to take on the perspective of others—to enter their emotional, perceptual, and social worlds. Under certain circumstances, empathy can be cultivated into a skill, rendering it a tool more controlled and consciously applied. Inherent in all this are two distinct modes of empathy: easy and difficult empathy. The former, often seen as perilous for the judiciary, can lead to unfiltered reactions, sentimentality, overidentification, and bias. Judges often associate it with a loss of impartiality. In contrast, the latter mode impacts judicial processes positively by bolstering fact-finding and fostering procedural justice. However, development of this mode and its incorporation into the judicial role are dependent on structural, organizational, and cultural factors. Crucially, one of the empathy labor avenues, as interpreted from the views of the interviewed judges, entails a transition from empathy as an innate, unintentional response to empathy as a refined, intentional skill. This approach correlates naturally with the shift from easy to difficult empathy.

Another way of grasping the nuances entrenched in the territory of law and empathy is to draw another distinction, this time between different sets of circumstances. The first constitutes the situation in which judges empathize

DOI: 10.4324/9781003546580-8

with a party or parties while handling a case. This encompasses their emotional responses at all stages of the process: the courtroom hearings, the solitary moments while reading trial documents, and the reaching of a final verdict. This situation involves activation of what easy empathy, as an ability, brings. The second constitutes the situation in which judges employ judicial empathy—an acquired skill (or set of skills) that builds upon innate abilities but is molded to and embedded in the judicial ethos, value system, and obligations. Here, an entering into the emotional, perceptual, and social world of another person is a competency structured, polished, and adapted to the specific judicial setting. Judicial empathy facilitates a show of recognition and respect for all parties involved, consideration for what participants might be feeling or thinking in order to protect their rights, attentiveness while signaling patience and commitment, and transcension of one's initial impressions through an openness to the narratives of others.

This differentiation—between using empathy as a natural ability and employing judicial empathy as a skill—is something we aimed to distill from interviews during which we guided judges in Poland to recount and expound upon their views and experiences. However, the justices with whom we conversed in the early 2020s often lacked self-reflexivity as well as the conceptual terminology enabling them to articulate this clearly. Most, thinking in terms of easy empathy, expressed reservations about using it in the judicial realm; concurrently, however, they explored and approved the phenomenon that is judicial empathy.

A crucial specificity of the latter (also perfectly illustrating its nature) is that while easy empathy is always triggered by some concrete stimulus in the moment, judicial empathy is rooted in judges' long-developed experience and expectations about what others might feel, think, and see in the social world. Those expectations have been shaped by the institutional nature of their work environment and the repetitiveness of certain states of affairs. For example, several of the interviewed judges developed detailed protocols for welcoming newcomers in the courtroom at the start of a hearing, a welcome consisting of rehearsed verbal statements accompanied by nonverbal messaging. This strategy stems from generalized thinking by judges about how others might feel and experience certain (often new) situations and represents a getting into the perspective of particular categories of people involved in a court proceeding. From this angle, empathy—or rather judicial empathy—can even be seen as a trivial yet obviously needed component of the professionalism of judges.

Following the broader discussion on the role and integration of empathy into judicial practice, several of our concrete findings should be highlighted.

First, the subject of empathy is not easy for judges to discuss, as they are not trained to focus on elements related to empathic as well as emotional responses. Typically, these topics fall outside their immediate concerns, and it would be naïve to expect judges to provide a comprehensive theorization of empathy's role in their work. Importantly, the environment in which Polish judges operate does not encourage self-reflection on their decision-making processes. Several judges expressed gratitude after the interviews for being given a safe space to ponder their inner thought processes. Therefore, it is crucial to create work environments for judges that foster opportunities for self-awareness and reflexivity regarding their reasoning and decisions. Such spaces would help anchor a skill-based approach that integrates these aspects as essential elements in a judge's professional development.

This topic requires more commentary. Skill development can result from deliberate, intentional efforts, but also from habitual practices shaped by the social (professional) environment. The process of embedding a controlled empathy into the judicial role can happen even without the conscious effort of judges. In fact, intuitive tendencies function in concert with a judge's reflective and rational capacities to develop precisely this skillset. In either case, factors such as the adequacy of prior legal education and subsequent judicial training—not to mention the workload, administration and regulation of the courts, and overall sociopolitical context—do impact the scale and intensity of a maturation of empathic impulses and other competencies among judges. The lack of institutionalized opportunities prompting self-reflection within the judicial role—in conjunction with the extensive ritualization of court procedures and the factory-like organization of assignments and assessments thereof—diverts judges' attention away from focused efforts aimed at their own development. Hence, establishing conditions that create space for growth and progression over a judge's career should be a crucial objective for those organizing and supervising the judiciary.

A second finding is that, generally speaking, Polish judges present a more optimistic stance regarding the actual and desired role of empathy in their work than one would expect when met with the stone-faced demeanor informed by Poland's tradition of legal positivism. Interestingly, the interviewees unanimously acknowledged that empathy, to varying degrees and at different stages, does play a role in their determinations. Where they differ strongly is precisely the stage at which they situate their empathic acts. This suggests that judges from civil law jurisdictions do not significantly differ from their common law counterparts, who also recognize empathy as an essential (albeit not the most important) skill for judges. It might be speculated that the broader range of responsibilities and tasks undertaken by civil law justices provides more opportunities to exercise empathy. While our research project sample was not representative, we employed an in-depth interview guide designed to minimize bold, practiced, or sweeping statements. Ultimately, the line of thinking, opinions, and use of empathy by the Polish judges was, by and large, cut of the same cloth; noteworthy variances emerged only among the family court division judges.

The third result is that this more favorable view of empathy implies neither an overoptimism nor a conviction that empathy is at the core of a judge's work. It does, however, spotlight empathy's role more significantly than previously imagined. Still, this did not constitute blind acceptance: The judges did acknowledge the limits of empathy. They noted, in particular, the risks associated with easy empathy, such as excessive emotionality, overidentification with parties, and compromised impartiality and neutrality. In all cases, the justices expressed an overriding skepticism about, or even opposition toward, words and actions reflecting uncontrolled, unmanaged empathy. Thus, whereas it was recognized as important, the judges remained cautious about the application of empathy in providing final judgments. The interviewees heeded professional standards of impartiality, but did not see fundamental problems in merging empathy with impartiality. However, assertions by the judges in our cohort that empathy does not jeopardize impartiality and, ultimately, that the rationality of judgments did not align with the view that empathic skills—especially those related to active listening and open-mindedness—can, in fact, play a part in ensuring impartiality.

A fourth notable point to consider is the overconfidence that some (or even most) judges exhibited regarding their ability to rein in their reactions, control internal processes, and fend off potential bias. Many judges voiced little concern for the unintended consequences of uncontrolled empathy, particularly when feeling empathy toward individuals similar to themselves or sharing similar experiences. Since, in abstract conjecture, they recognized the dangers of easy empathy, the interviewees were quick to emphasize their self-control over these impulses; they often downplayed the subconscious impact that emotions and other triggers might have on their decision-making. Quite interestingly, the judges in our sample tended to attribute potential problems more to others' perceptions of judicial bias than to their own internal vulnerabilities. This kind of apologia constituted, paradoxically, further evidence of a dearth of self-critical and honest reflection upon the difficulties of effectively managing psychological reactions.

The fifth observation was that judges did not associate their use of empathy with any explicit legal concepts or principles. In theory, such a connection should be possible: Certain procedural principles might correspond with perspective-taking, getting into the position of another individual. Indeed, references to procedural justice, particularly in the classic Tylorian sense, can be traced in the judges' narratives: This is discernable at moments in which our interviewees highlighted how courtroom participants felt about the way they were treated during a trial. Notably, this was not associated with easy empathy, but rather mirrored expectations shaped by prior experiences and situational demands.

Sixth, the singularity of family law adjudication and its impact on the way empathy is dealt with in the narrative of family division judges are additional general findings to be emphasized. Family judges are aware of the unique nature of their specialization, the distinctive types of cases handled in family divisions, and, most importantly, the need to employ a greater degree of empathy, often with a more emotional component. This stands in contrast to judges working in other legal areas, who tend to distance themselves from emotional language and rhetoric, expressing greater caution when discussing empathy. Family judges admitted openly and frankly that empathy plays a significant role in their work.

Finally, in closing, the vital role that language plays in shaping social reality needs also to be noted. While the interviewed judges may not have always used the term directly, their frequent touching on empathy themes in their narratives suggests that, even if unconsciously and encrypted in verse, the focal point was empathy. All in all, although empathy itself is not yet a word widely used or a concept broadly applied—in legal studies in general or the judiciary in particular—it does have a performative effect. And that, in turn, could alter how both society and judges themselves understand the judiciary and its role in delivering justice.

Index

For Product Safety Concerns and Information please contact our EU representative GPSR@taylorandfrancis.com
Taylor & Francis Verlag GmbH, Kaufingerstraße 24, 80331 München, Germany

www.ingramcontent.com/pod-product-compliance
Lightning Source LLC
LaVergne TN
LVHW021130300926
849160LV00010B/947